Process Consultation
Volume I

Second Edition

Process Consultation
Volume I

*Its Role in
Organization Development*

Edgar H. Schein
*Sloan School of Management,
Massachusetts Institute of Technology*

▼▲ **Addison-Wesley Publishing Company**
*Reading, Massachusetts • Menlo Park, California • New York
Don Mills, Ontario • Wokingham, England • Amsterdam • Bonn
Sydney • Singapore • Tokyo • Madrid • San Juan*

This book is in the Addison-Wesley Series on Organization Development. Editors: Edgar H. Schein, Richard Beckhard

Other titles in the series:

Organizational Transitions: Managing Complex Change, Second Edition
Richard Beckhard and Reuben Harris

Organization Development: A Normative View
W. Warner Burke

Team Building: Issues and Alternatives, Second Edition
William G. Dyer

The Technology Connection: Strategy and Change in the Information Age
Marc S. Gerstein

Power and Organization Development: Mobilizing Power to Implement Change
Larry E. Greiner and Virginia E. Schein

Designing Organizations for High Performance
David P. Hanna

Stream Analysis: A Powerful Way to Diagnose and Manage Organizational Change
Jerry I. Porras

Process Consultation, Volume II: Lessons for Managers and Consultants
Edgar H. Schein

Managing Conflict: Interpersonal Dialogue and Third-Party Roles, Second Edition
Richard E. Walton

Library of Congress Cataloging-in-Publication Data
(Revised for vol. 1)

Schein, Edgar H.
   Process consultation.

   (Addison-Wesley series: organization development)
(v. 1: Addison-Wesley series on organization development)
   Includes bibliographies.
   Contents: v. 1 Its role in organization development—[v. 2] Lessons for managers and consultants.
   1. Business consultants.   2. Social psychology.
I. Title.   II. Series: Addison-Wesley series : organization development.   III. Series: Addison-Wesley series on organization development.

HD69.C6S28   658.4'6   76-91149
ISBN 0-201-06736-6 (v. 1)

16 17 18 19 20 BA 95

Foreword

The Addison-Wesley Series on Organization Development originated in the late 1960s when a number of us recognized that the rapidly growing field of "OD" was not well understood or well defined. We also recognized that there was no one OD philosophy, and hence one could not at that time write a textbook on the theory and practice of OD, but one could make clear what various practitioners were doing under that label. So the original six books by Beckhard, Bennis, Blake and Mouton, Lawrence and Lorsch, Schein, and Walton launched what has since become a continuing enterprise. The essence of this enterprise was to let different authors speak for themselves instead of trying to summarize under one umbrella what was obviously a rapidly growing and highly diverse field.

By 1981 the series included nineteen titles, having added books by Beckhard and Harris, Cohen and Gadon, Davis, Dyer, Galbraith, Hackman and Oldham, Heenan and Perlmutter, Kotter, Lawler, Nadler, Roeber, Schein, and Steele. This proliferation reflected what had happened to the field of OD. It was growing by leaps and bounds, and it was expanding into all kinds of organizational areas and technologies of intervention. By this time many textbooks existed as well that tried to capture the core concepts of the field, but we felt that diversity and innovation were still the more salient aspects of OD today.

The present series is an attempt both to recapture some basics and to honor the growing diversity. So we have begun a series of revisions of some of the original books and have added a set of new authors or old authors with new content. Our hope is to capture the spirit of inquiry and innovation that has always been the hallmark of organization development and to launch with these books a new wave of insights into the forever tricky problem of how to change and improve organizations.

We are grateful that Addison-Wesley has chosen to continue the series and are also grateful to the many reviewers who have helped us and the authors in the preparation of the current series of books.

Cambridge, Massachusetts   Edgar H. Schein
New York, New York   Richard Beckhard

Preface

This book was originally written to communicate to my academic colleagues what I did when I went off to work with a company and to describe for consultants and managers my view of important events that occurred in organizations. It is only in retrospect, after some two decades of working as a process consultant, that I can see more clearly the philosophical and attitudinal assumptions that underlie this approach.

When I started out I was learning what seemed to work best. As I look back, I realize that there are some very important reasons why process consultation works, and these reasons — the assumptions underlying process consultation — have stood the test of time.

In revising this book, therefore, I have tried to stay close to the original formulations. I have added material only where it seemed to enhance the original theme. My thinking has, of course, evolved somewhat as a result of continued experience both with the consultation model and with the original version of this book. For example, I have found that this approach to working with people is highly relevant not only to consultants but to managers themselves. Many of the most enthusiastic readers of this book have been managers. I therefore also wrote a second volume that articulates the same basic philosophy and attitude but directs them more pointedly at the managerial audience and refines the concepts presented here further (Schein, 1987a). I had originally planned to incorporate all of these ideas into the revision of this book, but that would have made it double in length and destroyed the integrity that this book has had. The reader who wants to get a quick overview of the assumptions, foci, and methods of PC can get all of that in this revised volume 1. The reader who is interested enough to consider how this really works out in practice, what its pitfalls and problems are, and what additional theories and models are needed to fully understand the vicissitudes of PC should go on to volume II.

The decision to revise this book and the planning of how to do it were greatly facilitated by my colleague Marc Gerstein, who offered many helpful ideas on what to preserve and what to change. I am grateful to Addison-Wesley for having revived the entire OD series, and am, as usual, greatly indebted to my colleague and co-editor, Richard Beckhard. My students and clients have been most helpful in sharpening the ideas presented here.

Sherie Potts was most helpful in the difficult chore of getting a text that had been prepared in the technological dark ages of typewriting onto a word processor so that editing would be easier. Also, in the frantic effort to get this book to press on time, not only did I have the emotional support of my wife, Mary, but she even pitched in on the typing and editing.

Cambridge, Massachusetts   E.H.S.

Contents

Part I
Process Consultation Defined

In this part the basic concept of process consultation is defined and compared to other major consultation concepts. It is emphasized that process consultation is a kind of philosophy about and attitude toward the process of helping individuals, groups, and organizations. It is not merely a set of techniques to be compared to and contrasted with other techniques.

Process consultation underlies the broader concept of organization development and is the key philosophical underpinning to organization development in that most of what the consultant does in helping organizations is based on the assumptions of process consultation. Understanding such assumptions is therefore critical to understanding the broader concept of organization development.

1

What Is Process Consultation?

This book is about a special kind of consultation that I am calling *process consultation* (PC). I will describe what it is and what role it plays in organization development (OD).

In focusing on process consultation I will be looking at one of the key activities that go on at the beginning of (and throughout) any OD effort. OD is typically defined as a planned organizationwide kind of program, but its component parts are usually activities that the consultant carries out with individuals or groups, and the attitudes with which these activities are carried out reflect the assumptions that underlie PC.

This volume will focus on these kinds of activities and, therefore, will deal primarily with interpersonal and group events. More important than the focus of such activities, however, are the attitude and philosophy that underlie the consultant's behavior vis-à-vis the client and pervade all aspects of any OD program.

I will not try to give an overview of OD programs as a whole, but will focus on the process by which the consultant builds readiness for change, actually conducts training as part of the OD effort, and works with the key individuals of an organization as part of an OD program, always attempting to illustrate the importance of the attitude that the consultant takes toward the helping process.

The field of consultation has grown remarkably in recent years, yet there is still conceptual confusion about what a consultant actually does for an organization, how he[1] goes about doing it, and what his assumptions are about giving help. For example, does the consultant provide information, analyze information using special diagnostic tools, help clients to diagnose complex problems, give managers support and comfort, recommend solutions to organizational problems, help managers to implement difficult or unpopular decisions, or some or all of these in various combinations?

Many analyses of the consultation process argue that unless the client manager knows exactly what he is looking for from the consultant, he is likely to be sorely disappointed. In reality, however, the manager often does not know what he is looking for and indeed should not really be expected to know. All he knows is that something is not working right and he needs some kind of help. An important part of any consultation process, then, must be to help the manager or the organization to figure out what the problem is, and only then decide what further kind of help is needed.

Managers often sense that all is not well or that things could be better, but they do not have the tools with which to translate their vague feelings into concrete action steps. The kind of consultation I will attempt to describe in this book deals with problems of this sort. Process consultation does not assume that the manager knows what is wrong, or what is needed, or what the consultant should do. The only thing required for the process to begin constructively is some *intent* on the part of someone in the organization to improve the way it is operating. The consultation process itself then helps the manager to define diagnostic steps that lead ultimately to action programs and concrete changes that improve the situation.

Process consultation is a difficult concept to describe sim-

---

[1]To simplify the writing I will use "he" whenever I refer to consultants or clients in general with the understanding that this is not intended as a sexist reference.

ply and clearly. It does not lend itself to a simple definition or to the giving of a few illustrative examples, because it is more of a philosophy or a set of underlying assumptions about the helping process that lead the consultant to take a certain kind of attitude toward his relationship with the client.

I will try to give some perspective to these assumptions by contrasting PC with some other consultation models. Then I will provide some historical perspective to indicate why PC is an increasingly relevant activity in today's organizational world, and why it is particularly relevant to OD efforts. Finally, I will devote the bulk of this volume to the actual procedure of PC: what the consultant looks for, how the process starts, how a relationship with the client is developed, what kinds of interventions are made at various stages, how the process is evaluated, and how it is terminated.[2]

Models of Consultation

Consultation processes can be distinguished best by looking at the assumptions they make about the client, the nature of help, and the role of the consultant. Three basic models can be identified.

1. The Purchase of Expertise Model

The most prevalent model of consultation is certainly the purchase of expert information or an expert service. The buyer, usually an individual manager or some group in the organization, defines a need and concludes that the organization has neither the resources nor the time to fulfill that need. He will then look to a consultant to provide the information or the service.

For example: (1) A manager may wish to know how a particular group of consumers feels, or how a group of employees will react to a new personnel policy, or what the state of morale

---

[2]In volume 2 of *Process Consultation* (1987) more detail is given on how the consultant makes his moment-to-moment decisions as he works with the client and what underlying concepts are relevant to an understanding of the consulting process.

is in a given department. (2) The manager may wish to know how to organize a particular group and may need the consultant to find out how other companies organize such groups, for example, how to organize the accounting and control system given the capabilities of current information technology. (3) The manager may wish to know particular things about competitor companies, such as their marketing strategy, how much of the price of their product is determined by production costs, how they organize their research and development function, how many employees they have in a typical plant, and so on.

In each of these cases there is an assumption that the manager knows what kind of information or service he is looking for. The likelihood that this model will work then depends on

1. whether or not the manager has correctly diagnosed his own needs;
2. whether or not he has correctly communicated those needs to the consultant;
3. whether or not he has accurately assessed the capabilities of the consultant to provide the information or the service;
4. whether or not he has thought through the consequences of having the consultant gather such information, and/or the consequences of implementing changes that may be recommended by the consultant.

The frequent dissatisfaction with consultants and the low rate of implementation of their recommendations can easily be explained when one considers how many assumptions have to be met for the purchase model to work effectively.

Process consultation, in contrast, involves the manager and the consultant in a period of *joint diagnosis*. The consultant is willing to come into the organization without a clear mission or goal because of an underlying assumption that any organization can improve its processes and become more effective if it can accurately locate those processes that make a difference to its overall performance. No organizational structure or process is perfect. Every organization has strengths and weaknesses. Therefore, the manager who senses that "something" is wrong because performance or morale is not what it should be *should not* leap into action until he has a clear idea of the strengths and weaknesses of the present structures and processes. The main goal of the process consultant is to help the manager to make such a diagnosis and to develop a valid action plan for himself. The importance of joint diagnosis derives from the fact that the consultant can seldom learn enough about any given organization to really know what a better course of action would be or even what information would really help them most, because the members of the organization perceive, think about, and react to information in terms of their traditions, values, and assumptions, that is, their organizational culture (Schein, 1985) and the particular styles and personalities of their key members.

However, the consultant can help the manager (1) to become a sufficiently good diagnostician himself, and (2) to learn how to manage organizational processes better so that he can solve problems for himself. It is a crucial assumption of the PC philosophy that problems will stay solved longer and be solved more effectively if the organization solves those problems itself. The consultant has a role in teaching diagnostic and problem-solving skills, but he should not attempt actually to solve the problems himself.

2. The Doctor–Patient Model

Another common consultation model is that of "doctor–patient." One or more managers in the organization decide to bring in a consultant to "check them over," to discover if there are any organizational areas that are not functioning properly and might need attention. Or the manager may detect symptoms of ill health, such as dropping sales, high numbers of customer complaints, or quality problems, but not know how to make a diagnosis of what is causing the problems.

The consultant is brought into the organization to find out what is wrong with which part of the organization and then, like the physician, recommend a program of therapy or prescribe a remedial measure. This model puts a great deal of power into the hands of the consultant in that he both diagnoses and prescribes, and is therefore a model that appeals to consultants.

As most readers will recognize from their own experience, this model is fraught with difficulties in spite of its popularity.

One of the most obvious difficulties is the assumption that the consultant can get accurate diagnostic information on his own. But the organizational unit that is defined as "sick" may be reluctant to reveal the kind of information that the consultant would need to make an accurate diagnosis. In fact, it is quite predictable that on questionnaires or in interviews systematic distortions will occur. The direction of these distortions will depend on the climate of the organization. If the climate is one of distrust and insecurity, the respondents will most likely hide any damaging information from the consultant because of fear of retaliation, something that we have seen repeatedly in the misadventures of whistle-blowers.

On the other hand, if the climate is one of high trust, respondents are likely to view contact with the consultant as an opportunity to get all their gripes off their chests, leading to an exaggeration of the problem. In either case, unless the consultant spends a lot of time observing the department, he is not likely to get an accurate picture of what may be going on.

An equally great difficulty with this model is that the client/patient is likely to be unwilling to believe the diagnosis or to accept the prescription offered by the consultant. I suspect that most organizations have drawers full of reports by consultants that are either not understood or not accepted by the "patient." What is wrong, of course, is that the "doctor" has not built up a common diagnostic frame of reference with his client. If the consultant does all the diagnosing while the client/manager waits passively for a prescription, it is predictable that a communication gulf will arise that will make the prescription seem either irrelevant or unpalatable.

Even in medicine, doctors have increasingly realized that patients do not automatically accept diagnoses and do what the doctor recommends. One sees this most clearly in the cross-cultural context, where assumptions about illness or what one does about it may differ from our own, but one also sees it, for example, in the treatment of breast cancer where the oncologist has to involve the patient in the crucial choice as to whether to have a radical mastectomy or a program of chemotherapy and radiation. Similarly, in plastic surgery or in the decision of whether or not to have back surgery, the patient's goals and self-image become crucial variables in determining the ultimate success of the surgery.

In other words, the success of the doctor–patient model will depend on

1. whether or not the initial client has accurately identified which person, group, or department is, in fact, "sick";
2. whether or not the "patient" will reveal accurate information;
3. whether or not the "patient" will accept and believe the diagnosis that the "doctor" arrives at;
4. whether or not the "patient" will accept the prescription, that is, do what the "doctor" recommends.

Process consultation, in contrast, focuses on joint diagnosis and the passing on to the client of the consultant's diagnostic skills. The consultant may recognize early in his work what some of the problems are in the organization and how they might be solved. But he does not share his insights prematurely, for two reasons. One, he may be wrong. If he prematurely makes a diagnosis that is incorrect, he may damage his credibility with the client and undermine the relationship. Two, he recognizes that even if he is right, the client may well be defensive, may not listen or may wish to deny what he hears, or may misunderstand what the consultant is saying and thus subvert remedial efforts.

It is a key assumption underlying PC that the client must learn to see the problem for himself by sharing in the diagnostic process and be actively involved in generating a remedy. The consultant may play a key role in helping to sharpen the diagnosis and may provide suggestions for alternate remedies that may not have occurred to the client. But he encourages the client to make the ultimate decision on what remedy to apply.

Again, the consultant does this on the assumption that if he teaches the client to diagnose and remedy situations himself, problems will be solved more permanently and the client will have learned the skills necessary to solve new problems as they arise.

It should also be emphasized that the process consultant may or may not be an expert at solving the particular problems that may be uncovered. The important point in PC is that such expertise is less relevant than are the skills of involving the client in self-diagnosis and helping him to find a remedy that fits his particular situation and his unique set of needs. The process consultant must be an expert at giving help and at establishing a relationship with clients that makes it possible to be helpful. He does not need to be an expert in marketing, finance, or strategy. If problems are uncovered in such areas, the consultant can help the client to find an expert resource and, more important, help the client to think through how best to ensure that he will get the help he needs from those experts.

3. The Process Consultation Model
and Its Underlying Assumptions

The main assumptions of what I am calling the process consultation philosophy or model can now be summarized:

1. Clients/managers often do not know what is wrong and need special help in diagnosing what their problems actually are.
2. Clients/managers often do not know what kinds of help consultants can give to them; they need to be helped to know what kinds of help to seek.
3. Most clients/managers have a constructive intent to improve things, but they need help in identifying what to improve and how to improve it.
4. Most organizations can be more effective than they are if they learn to diagnose and manage their own strengths and weaknesses. No organizational form is perfect; hence every form of organization will have some weaknesses for which compensatory mechanisms must be found.
5. A consultant probably cannot, without exhaustive and time-consuming study or actual participation in the client organization, learn enough about the culture of the organization to suggest reliable new courses of action. Therefore, unless remedies are worked out jointly with members of the organization who do know what will and will not work in their culture, such remedies are

likely either to be wrong or to be resisted because they come from an outsider.

6. Unless the client/manager learns to see the problem for himself and thinks through the remedy, he will not be willing or able to implement the solution and, more important, will not learn how to fix such problems should they recur. The process consultant can provide alternatives, but decision making about such alternatives must remain in the hands of the client.

7. The essential function of PC is to pass on the skills of how to diagnose and fix organizational problems so that the client is more able to continue on his own to improve the organization.

Process Consultation Defined

With these assumptions in mind, we can define PC:

PC is a set of activities on the part of the consultant that help the client to perceive, understand, and act upon the process events that occur in the client's environment in order to improve the situation as defined by the client.

The process consultant seeks to give the client insight into what is going on around him, within him, and between him and other people. Based on such insight, the consultant then helps the client to figure out what he should do about the situation. But the core of this model is that the client must be helped to remain "pro-active," in the sense of retaining both the diagnostic and remedial initiative. Allowing the client to become dependent on the consultant, as comfortable as that may be for both parties, is a prescription for failure in the helping process if complex human systems processes are involved.

The events to be observed and learned from are the human actions that occur in the normal flow of work, in the conduct of meetings, in the formal or informal encounters between members of the organization, and in the more formal organizational structures. Of particular relevance are the client's own actions and their impact on other people in the organization.

Implicit in this model is the further assumption that all organizational problems are fundamentally problems involving human interactions and processes. No matter what technical, financial, or other matters may be involved, there will always be humans involved in the design and implementation of such other processes. A thorough understanding of human processes and the ability to improve such processes are therefore fundamental to any organizational improvement.

As long as organizations are networks of people engaged in achieving some common goals, there will be various kinds of processes occurring between them. Therefore, the more we understand about how to diagnose and improve such processes, the greater will be our chances of finding solutions to the more technical problems and of ensuring that such solutions will be accepted and used by members of the organization.

Part II

Human Processes and How to Intervene in Them

In this part of the book I will review the major human processes that I have observed to be relevant to helping organizations improve their effectiveness. In the first chapter I will provide some historical perspective, and in each subsequent chapter I will analyze a major human process, such as communication or leadership, and highlight what the process consultant would observe and what he then might do about what he observes, that is, how he might intervene.

Not all possible human processes are analyzed, and in each case only the most relevant aspects of each process are described. The descriptions are often deliberate simplifications designed to make clear the underlying significance of what is going on.

Knowledge of how human processes work is essential for the consultant in order to diagnose the problems and select wisely the manner in which he intervenes. But even the process of observing and asking questions to find out what is going on constitutes interventions. So the consultant can never separate diagnostic and intervention activities in his behavior, even though these are conceptually distinct when we analyze the consultation process.

2

Human Processes
in Organizations:
An Overview

The study of human processes in organizations has been the direct result of improved techniques of observation and improved conceptual models of how processes in organizations affect ultimate outcomes. The key to understanding what makes an organization more or less effective is *how* it does things.

Organizations can be designed and structured in many different ways, each of which can be successful. If one is to understand why the same structures are successful at one time and unsuccessful at another, one must understand various processes — how goals are set, how the means to be used are determined, the forms of communication used among members, their processes of problem solving and decision making, how they run meetings and groups, how superiors and subordinates relate to each other, and ultimately how leaders lead.

The process consultant must be conversant in each of these areas, to be able both to observe such processes and to intervene effectively in them. In this chapter I will provide an overview and a road map. In subsequent chapters I will discuss each of the major processes in detail and provide some intervention tools to aid in improving those processes.

Structure versus Process: A Historical Note

Early studies of organizations were dominated by the "scientific management" school of thought leading to an almost exclusive preoccupation with the structural or static elements of the organization. What should be the correct division of labor? What is the right span of control? Should the organization be structured by functions, such as sales and manufacturing; by product lines, such as trucks, large autos, and small autos; or by geography? How many levels should there be in the hierarchy? Should each department have its staff people, such as personnel, or should there be a single centralized staff?

This concern for organizational "statics" is understandable and partially appropriate, because organizations are open systems that exist in uncertain and dynamic environments. In order to survive they must stabilize some elements in the face of recurring disintegrative pressures from the environment. Just as total societies develop a culture, social structure, laws, and traditions as a way of stabilizing themselves, so organizations must find ways to conserve and stabilize their culture and structure (Schein, 1985).

The appeal of the structural approach is strong in the field of consultation. Management consulting firms are often brought in to examine the existing structure and to recommend alternative forms that are presumed to be more effective for achieving organizational goals. If the recommendations are acted on, reporting relationships are likely to be changed, departments are likely to be phased out or moved, jobs are redesigned or eliminated, and so on. To the extent that individual personalities are taken into account, they are also treated as static and structural factors to be worked around rather than changed.

The problem with this approach is twofold. Most serious is the possibility that the diagnosis will be incorrect or that the prescription for a new structure will ignore some major cultural or personality constraints, thus making the recommendations unimplementable. The report simply gets filed.

Less serious is the possibility that the diagnosis is correct but that the recommendations are incomplete because they ignore the human processes at work. The network of positions and roles that define the formal organizational structure is occupied by people, and those people in varying degrees put their own personalities into getting the job done. Not only does each role occupant have a certain style of doing his own work, but he has his own unique way of relating to other people in the organization. These processes of relating to others have a decisive influence on outcomes and must themselves become objects of diagnosis and intervention if any organization improvement is to occur.

Paradoxically, some processes recur with such regularity that they become virtually part of the structure. An authoritarian entrepreneur who always barks orders and expects instant obedience creates a militaristic form of organization that expresses, both in its formal structure and in the daily behavior of its managers, recurring patterns of top-down influence, unwillingness to accept suggestions from subordinates, ruthless disciplinary processes, and so on. But the consultant should make a clear distinction in his own head between structure in terms of formally defined positions and roles, and structure in terms of observed regularities of behavior. Structured *processes* are very much the domain of the process consultant.

Some Historical Roots

The study of organizational processes has several roots. One of these roots is the field of group dynamics as developed originally under the leadership of Kurt Lewin (1947). A second root was the development of systematic techniques for studying small-group processes such as those developed by Chapple (1940) in applied anthropology, Bales (1950, 1979) in sociology, and Carter et al. (1951) in psychology.

The classical experiments by White and Lippitt (1953) on the effects of different kinds of leadership showed that group productivity and morale were very much affected by the leadership style of the formal leader. Bales, in his extensive and detailed analyses of small-group problem solving, showed that groups developed certain patterns of behavior that were quite predictable. For example, two kinds of leader tended to emerge: a task leader who helps the group to do its job, and a "socioemotional" leader who helps to build and maintain good relations among group members. Only rarely were these two kinds of leader the same person in the groups studied. Such experiments showed that it was possible to study group processes and that such research would pay off in finding nonobvious regularities in such human processes.

A third, and closely related, historical root was the development of group dynamics and leadership training associated with the National Training Laboratories (Bradford et al., 1964; Schein and Bennis, 1965). Deriving from Lewinian concepts of action research, a technology of group observation and intervention in group processes has been developed over the last thirty-five years. This approach represents the most important precursor to PC in that most of the assumptions PC makes in relation to working with an organization are derived from assumptions that group "trainers" make in working with laboratory-training groups. For example, the trainer sees himself not as a teacher or an expert but as someone who helps group members to discover the kinds of events that are occurring in the group and the effects such events are having on themselves and other members.

A fourth root is the study of group relations and interpersonal processes in industrial organizations. These studies — originating in the early works of Mayo, Roethlisberger, and Dickson; carried forward by Arensberg, Whyte, Homans, and others who studied the "informal" organization in industry; and taken to the management ranks in works such as Melville Dalton's (1959) — showed that *how people actually relate to each other* bears only a limited similarity to *how the formal organization structure says they should behave* (Schein, 1965, 1980). These studies more than any others illustrate the need to study human processes in organizations by actual observation rather than to accept at face value what people say in interviews or on survey questionnaires.

Finally, an important root has been the work of Muzapher Sherif et al. (1961), who showed that regularities could be demonstrated not only within small groups but also between groups, and thus opened up the whole area of intergroup relations. For example, the perceptions, feelings, and behavior of people when they are in an intergroup competition are sufficiently predictable that one can readily create a demonstration exercise that reproduces those phenomena within a period of a couple of hours (Blake and Mouton, 1961).

As can be seen, PC is anchored deeply in social psychology, sociology, and anthropology. The understanding of and intervention into human processes in organizations require not merely an attitude or a decision to pay attention to such processes but also a good deal of knowledge of what to look for, how to look for it, how to interpret it, and what to do about it. Helping an organization to do its own diagnosis and to solve its own problems requires, in addition, helping skills that can be acquired only with experience in a training, clinical, or consulting role.

What Human Processes in Organizations Are More Relevant?

In the next several chapters I will describe what are in my view the most important processes that the process consultant must know something about. Some of these deal with face-to-face relationships between two or more people, some deal with groups and intergroup situations, and some are more broad organizational issues, such as norms, culture, and leadership.

This is not intended to be an exhaustive treatment of interpersonal, group, and organizational processes. Instead I have tried to select those processes that most often catch my attention when I am trying to be helpful. I will describe each area in simple, straightforward language that not only makes sense to me but communicates well to the layman. These can be thought of as "simplifying models" that capture the essence of the phenomena.

In the consultant role I have often found it necessary to translate difficult psychological ideas into simple formulations. In that process one sometimes has to sacrifice rigor, but as long as one knows what the underlying theory and research findings are, it is worthwhile to translate concepts into something the client can understand and deal with. By the same token, the layman not familiar with the underlying theory or the research on which some of the points rest should be cautious in using these concepts in his efforts to be helpful.

The concepts to be reviewed will be illustrated whenever

possible from my own consulting experience and will generally mirror the most critical events as they occur chronologically in the consulting process. Many of the illustrations come from group events because most often the process consultant finds himself in one or another group situation, but this in no way implies that PC is primarily a group-oriented process. Rather, PC is characterized more by the attitude toward the helping process that one takes, as I will try to show.

To recap, PC is characterized by the desire and skill on the part of the consultant to create a relationship with the client (1) that the client will regard as helpful, (2) that will enable the client to focus on the critical process events in his own environment, and (3) will enable the client to diagnose and intervene in those processes to make his organization more effective.

3

Communication Processes

One of the most important basic processes in organizations, and one of the easiest to observe, is how people communicate with each other, particularly in face-to-face and small-group situations. The process consultant must be aware of such processes because they are central to the establishment of his relationship with the client in the one-on-one situation, and they are likely to be the most salient aspect of the kinds of settings in which he will find himself early in the relationship.

For example, if I decide to get involved with a client, I am likely, following the initial contact, to find myself with several members of the client organization at a group meeting with the opportunity to observe what goes on between them. Not only have I observed my own communication with the client so far, but I can now observe how different members in the client organization communicate with each other.

Many formulations of communication depict it as a simple problem of transfer of information from one person to another. But, as we all know, the process is anything but simple, and the information transferred is often highly variable and highly complex. We communicate facts, feelings, perceptions, innuendos, and various other things all in the same "simple" message. We communicate not only through the spoken and written word but through facial expressions, gestures, physical posture, tone of voice, timing of when we speak, what we do not say, and so on. The present chapter will start with simple observables about communication and then will move into deeper, less observable communication processes.

Who Communicates? How Often? For How Long?

The easiest analysis of communication is to focus only on the *relative frequency* and *duration* of communication acts. Thus, if the process consultant wishes to observe the communication behavior of a group or committee, he can list the names of all the members and put a check mark next to a name each time that person says something. He can measure duration by putting down a check mark every few seconds as long as the speaker continues.

After some period of time the chart can be summarized to show who has talked, how often, and how much of the total available time he has used. One can also determine who used short communications and who spoke for long periods. If one wanted to analyze written communications, an analogous chart could be set up to determine who sends, how often he sends, and how long the message is.

I have deliberately ignored such factors as the content of the message in order to illustrate that even very simple things can be observed and learned from. For example, in my experience both in training groups and in meetings, a frequent occurrence is that one or more "quiet" members are accused by the more vocal ones of not contributing their thoughts to the discussion. In many instances I have heard the "quiet" members deny this accusation, saying that they had been talking but that apparently no one had been listening to them.

To help the group to focus on this kind of issue, having a record of how many times each person actually spoke relative to other persons can be extremely valuable. In most instances I have found that the "silent" member is quite right; he had spoken several times but others had stereotyped him as silent and hence not heard what he had to say. Once the facts are recognized, it is possible to move on to the more important issue of *why* some members are listened to more than others.

It should be noted that the process consultant helps the group by gathering data, but when and how he uses these data will depend very much on his judgment of how ready the group is to look at its own process. The key assumption *always* is that the group or the individual manager who is the client must collaborate in formulating the diagnosis; nothing is gained by a premature feedback of data that will be either ignored or resisted. The most common intervention the process consultant therefore makes early in the consultation process is to remain silent, to ask questions if he is not clear about something that is going on, or simply to make generally encouraging remarks.

Even though the consultant may have made an extensive analysis of the group's communication patterns, he may withhold all of the data until he senses that the group is ready. Furthermore, sensing when the group is ready calls for a complex judgment based on other observations that I will describe below. The consultant cannot treat a simple request from the client as equivalent to being ready. All too often I have had a group ask for my observations of the group's process only to find, once I began to share them, that the group had trapped me in a position where I could be neutralized by being shown by some members how "wrong" my observations were.

Who Communicates to Whom?

The next level of complexity of observation would be to determine who talks or writes to whom. Such observation is not difficult with written communications, if they are addressed; it can be very tricky in a group situation, however, since people often are not explicit about to whom they are directing themselves. The observer may have to watch the speaker's eyes to see whom he is looking at when he is talking, or he may observe body posture for similar cues.

These observations, like the previous set, could be recorded in a matrix where all the members are listed on both the horizontal and vertical axes and a check mark is made in the appropriate cell of the matrix. Alternatively, the method could extend the previous one by simply listing for each communication who the speaker and who the recipients were.

This level of communication analysis can reveal a number of processes. For example, if one tracks who speaks to whom fairly carefully, one quickly discovers that some members talk to the whole group, some talk to the ceiling or floor, and some members have favorite audiences. Having identified, for example, the fact that Joe tends mostly to direct his comments at Jane, the question arises as to why this occurs, leading to a next level of observation of their behavior. At this next level it may turn out that Joe talks mostly to Jane because the latter tends to agree with everything the former says. A kind of subgroup or coalition exists within the larger group, which may have a variety of implications for the functioning of the total group.

Alternatively, I have found that sometimes people talk to those others from whom they expect the most opposition or resistance. Thus Joe may have learned that Jane is the member most likely to "shoot him down." He talks first to Jane to see whether he can expect to get his point past what he sees to be his toughest hurdle.

The above illustration highlights the fact that any given observation that the consultant makes does not mean anything very significant in and of itself. Rather, the observations of regularities and key events in group communication serve as a guide or a set of cues for progressively more meaningful questions that then determine new areas of observation. For example, if the manager of the group exhibits a bias in terms of whom he tends to talk to in his meetings, this fact by itself means relatively little. But if the consultant observes how the members who are and the members who are not talked to by the boss react to this behavior, he can formulate some important hypotheses about the functioning of the group.

Who Talks After Whom? Who Interrupts Whom?

Closely related to the issue of who talks to whom is the matter of who triggers whom and in what ways. I have noted in observing groups that there are clear patterns of triggering. Whenever John speaks the odds are pretty good that Sue will be the next to speak even if the remarks were not initially directed to her. Again, this may reflect either support or a desire to undo the point John has made. As every observant group member has noted many times, such undoing can take the most elaborately polite forms, yet it remains a "Yes, *but* . . . " reaction nevertheless. As one group member once put it, in his company examples of such encouragement or undoing are labeled "Attaboys" and "Yeabuts," and the norm is that it takes at least three attaboys to undo the damaging effect of one yeabut in the group discussion.

Sometimes this level of analysis seems trivial, superficial, and contrived. If the observer's analysis stopped at this level, it would indeed be insufficient. What we need to underline again is that the overt surface behavior provides the clues as to what is going on between the people beneath the surface. Such clues not only help the process consultant understand what is going on but are a visible manifestation to the members themselves. If the consultant's role is to set up a situation of shared diagnosis, he must concentrate on observables that are seen as readily by the clients as by him. One of the great problems of psychologically sophisticated consultants who forget their mission as defined here is that they correctly interpret to the group what is happening, but the interpretation is so far detached from observable behavior that the group members reject both it and the consultant.

Let us now turn to the other behavior mentioned in the heading above: who interrupts whom. Observing this type of communication behavior is important because it gives us clues as to how members perceive their own status or power in the group relative to the status or power of other members. It is a matter of common observation, and has been documented in careful studies of deference, that the person of higher rank, status, or power feels free to interrupt someone of lower rank. We generally let the boss finish his sentences more often than he lets us finish ours. In those instances where this trend seems not to hold, one often finds that the members feel themselves to be of equal status even though objectively their rank may be different. Even then they might be more careful in public than in private situations.

Assuming a working team of equals, what does it mean if the marketing manager often interrupts the production manager, but the reverse seldom occurs? The process consultant would ask himself whether there was in fact a status difference, or, if not, whether the marketing manager simply felt himself to be more important than the production manager. In the latter case, a fairly common kind of problem arises from the fact that the production manager begins to feel a loss of influence, to which he may react by starting to fight rather than continuing to work cooperatively.

Without insight on the part of either as to how they are signaling their feeling in overt communication acts, it is difficult for them to improve their working relationship. They can improve the relationship only if the consultant can create a situation where they discover for themselves how their self-perceptions, perceptions of each other, and subjective judgments about their own influence relative to others come out in overt behavior.

In general, I have observed that interrupting others is one of the more common and more destructive kinds of communication behavior. Most people have relatively little awareness of how often and how crudely they cut in on others, convinced that what they have to say is more important than what they believe the previous speaker would have continued to say. When this process is itself interrupted by a consultant intervention, it often turns out that the person who first interrupted did not in fact really understand what the previous speaker was trying to say. In his eagerness he was formulating his own thoughts rather than listening to what was said before him.

One of the unfortunate consequences of frequent interruption is that the group is likely to interpret this as a sign of lack of organization. The suggestion is usually made that the way to control interruptions and avoid having too many people talking at once is to give the chairman more power to cut people off, call on people, and generally establish order. This solution substitutes external discipline for internal control. It misdiagnoses the problem as one of organization rather than recognizing it as a lack of concern of the members for each other, resulting in insufficient listening. If the problem is one of listening, then the formal-chairmanship solution will not deal with the problem. Members will still not listen but will instead be busy formulating what they will say when called on to speak.

Communication Style

Communication style is intended to refer to a whole range of factors, such as whether the person is assertive, questioning, pedantic, or humorous; whether his tone of voice is loud, soft, grating, or melodious; whether he accompanies his words with gestures; and so on. Insofar as the process consultant is interested in member relations, he is less concerned about style as an indicator of underlying personality and more concerned about the possible effects of a given communication style on the people with whom the person communicates.

For example, I may notice that a person talks very loudly and assertively, causing others gradually to tune him out, yet he seems to be quite unaware that this is happening. He may even become aware of his declining influence in the group and yet remain unaware of what has caused this decline. He does not hear himself as loud and assertive. The other members of the group who are no longer paying attention to him are also in a trap. They may not be paying attention because of the communication *style* used by the speaker and yet erroneously feel it is the *content* of what he is saying that is failing to hold their interest. Communication in this situation cannot improve until both parties to the problem gain some insight into what they are doing and why they are doing it (for example, what cues they are sending and are reacting to).

Gestural Communication (Kinesics)

As anthropologists and linguists have known for some time, body posture, gestures, facial expressions, and other nonverbal behavior can and do become patterned according to the culture in which the person grew up. To the extent that they are patterned and have symbolic meanings, they can be understood just as clearly as verbal or written communication. Certain gestures, for example, reflect ethnic background. Careful analysis of films of people in spontaneous interaction has revealed that some groups (for example, first-generation Jewish immigrants) tend to accompany assertive words with forward-reaching, one-handed gestures, often described as "buttonholing." First-generation Italians, in contrast, tend to use both hands in gesturing and to rotate them outward rather than pointing toward the listener.

Hall, in his excellent book *The Silent Language* (1959), describes a whole range of culturally determined nonverbal cues that must be understood if the listener is to make correct interpretations of the speaker. For example, in every culture there is a kind of "ideal sphere" around a person. This "sphere" is the territory or space around a person that may not be violated unless you are on intimate terms with him, have some legitimate reason, or are deliberately and aggressively violating it. Two examples of violation are standing too close and touching. In countries where this normal distance is less than in America, the American is likely to feel uncomfortable because people are always crowding him in conversation or getting him into corners.

Systematic observations of postural and gestural behavior have been made by Birdwhistell (1961) using methods of analysis first developed in the field of linguistics. This field of analysis he calls *kinesics*. He has identified, for example, some of the nonverbal behavior associated with courtship patterns which is properly labeled as "preening." It can be observed that a young man, when he suddenly finds himself in the company of an attractive girl, will straighten his tie, pull up his socks, run his fingers through his hair, adopt a slightly more erect posture, and have a higher muscle tonus. If the girl similarly notices the young man and responds to him, she will also show higher muscle tonus, may flush slightly, stroke her hair, check her makeup, straighten her stockings, and sketchily rearrange her clothing (Scheflen, 1965).

Further postural and nonverbal cues are also associated with what Scheflen identified as stages of "positioning for courtship" and "actions of invitation." Since such cues are culturally learned, their meaning is clear to members of the same culture. Such cues are often called "body language" and can be meaningfully interpreted providing the sender and observer are using a common cultural frame of reference. But there is little evidence that body language has universal meaning.

Although methods of analysis of such complex gestures are still in their infancy, it is not too difficult to imagine that they could be used successfully in identifying cues that accompany aggressiveness, excessive deference, boredom, and various other feelings that are of great importance in group situations. In fact, I suspect that most experienced managers already rely on many such clues but do so unsystematically and without complete awareness of what it is on which they are relying.

Levels of Communication

So far I have discussed more or less manifest and easily observable communication events. In order to make some sense of these events and to understand more fully how members of any encounter react to each other, it is important to analyze less easily observable events. As background for this discussion, some psychological theory about the nature of communication is also relevant.

As most of us know from observation of our own behavior, not only do we tend to react to the manifest content of what another person says to us, but we interpret what he says and use various subtle clues to get at the real meaning of the message. Often the same message carries more than one meaning, both a manifest and a latent meaning. Occasionally these meanings tend to contradict each other. One simple example is the person who issues an invitation with the statement "Come over to our house anytime," but leaves it sufficiently ambiguous through his tone of voice that you realize he does not really want you to come and is merely being polite. Another example is in work teams, where it is not unusual for a person to argue against a proposal because he feels he has to be consistent with a previous position or defend a group he represents, but to argue in a way that lets others know he is privately prepared to be convinced and will go along eventually. Often we say one thing in order to save face but manage to communicate something else.

Double messages of this kind do not pose unusual difficulties because the sender is aware of them and can clarify misunder-standings. Greater difficulty arises from double messages that re-flect parts of the person of which he is unaware. To illustrate, it is useful to think of the person as having several parts, as depicted in Figure 3–1. Quadrant 1 in the figure represents those areas of the person of which he himself is aware and which he is willing to share with others: the "open self." Quadrant 2 represents those parts of himself of which he is aware, but which he is consciously and deliberately trying to conceal from others. Typical examples that come up if one asks a group to reveal anonymously some of the things they conceal from others are areas of insecurity that the person is ashamed to admit, feelings and impulses that he considers to be antisocial or inconsistent with his self-image, memories of events where he failed or showed up particularly badly against his own standards, and most important, feelings and reactions to other people that he feels would be impolite or hurtful to reveal.

For example, Jill might think that the boss made a terrible presentation at the key meeting, leading to loss of the sale, but equally might feel she must withhold this reaction and compli-ment the boss "in order not to hurt his feelings or make him mad." As we will see later, one of the key insights resulting from

2 Concealed self	1 Open self
4 Unknown self	3 Blind self

Figure 3–1
The Parts of a Person *

*J. Luft, "The Johari Window," *Hum. Rel. Tr. News* 5, 1961, pp. 6–7.

PC is understanding of how much valuable loss of communication results from conscious concealment of reactions to interpersonal events.

Quadrant 3 in the figure is the key one for this discussion. The "blind area" of the self refers to those things that we unconsciously conceal from ourselves yet which are part of us and are communicated to others. "I am *not* angry," says the boss in loud tones, purple-faced, as he slams his fist on the table. "These meetings are quite relaxing for me," says the executive as his hand trembles, his voice cracks, and he either has a third martini or tries unobtrusively to slip a tranquilizer into his mouth. "I do not care about the opinions of others," says the manager, but then he gets upset if others do not notice him or his work.

All of us have, in the process of growing up, been rewarded for being certain kinds of people and punished for being other kinds. The young boy learns that it is all right to have aggressive feelings but that it is not all right to feel fear or tenderness when with other boys. So he begins to reject feelings of tenderness as being not part of himself. He suppresses them or refuses to recognize them as his own when they occur. Yet they may be quite visible to other people. How often have we said of a gruff, tough man that he is really very tender? What we are saying is that we see tender behavior but that the person himself cannot see his own tender side and must continue to deny it by maintaining a gruff exterior. I have seen executives who became aggressive in direct proportion to the amount of tenderness they felt for the people around them; and I have seen women who became studiously considerate and tender in direct proportion to the amount of aggression they were feeling but unwilling to admit to themselves.

Each of us thus has feelings and traits that we feel are not part of us, and we are blind to the fact that we do communicate many such feelings to others. We may also be blind to the fact that some of the feelings we try to conceal do leak out.

Quadrant 4 consists of those parts of the person of which neither he nor others are aware. Examples would be truly unconscious and deeply repressed feelings and impulses, hidden talents or skills, potentialities, and so on. For our purposes this area is irrelevant.

Let us now consider two people in interaction with each other (Fig. 3-2) and analyze the implications of the different kinds of messages and different levels of communication that occur. Most communication occurs between the two open selves of the persons (Arrow A), and most popularized analyses of the communication process confine themselves to this level.

A second level of communication is the signals or meanings that we pick up from a person's blind self and which he is unaware of sending (Arrow B).

A third level of communication occurs when we deliberately reveal something that we ordinarily tend to conceal (Arrow C). Usually we think of this as "confiding" in someone or "leveling" if we are sharing reactions or feelings generated by immediate events.

Finally, there is a less common but no less important level

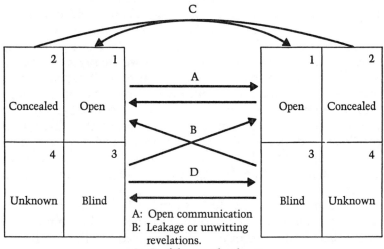

A: Open communication
B: Leakage or unwitting revelations.
C: Confiding or "leveling"
D: Emotional contagion

Figure 3-2
Types of Messages in a Two-Person Communication Situation

of communication, represented by Arrow D, which might best be labeled "emotional contagion." One person influences the feelings of another without either one's being consciously aware of the origin of the feeling. Sometimes the feeling that is aroused in the recipient mirrors that of the sender, as when tension that may be denied by the sender nevertheless makes the receiver tense as well. In other cases the feeling is different, as when a denied but displayed feeling in one person causes tension in the other because he does not know whether he should respond to the manifest level of communication (the denial of feeling) or to the latent level (the actually displayed feeling).

The process consultant must be aware of these subtleties and complications in levels of communication in order to understand fully the flow of interpersonal events. I have observed a group situation where the senior executive and chairman of the group became very angry at several members and punished them openly for failing to follow through on a project. Yet, surprisingly, he did not arouse any defensiveness or tensions on their part. The explanation was that they had learned over a long period of time that he was really frustrated over not being more involved in the project himself and was really communicating, without being aware of it, that he was feeling sorry for himself. His group reacted more to this second message and worked hard to involve him in the project. When they succeeded, his anger subsided. What this executive was unconsciously denying was his need to be involved and needed (a very tender feeling), yet these feelings were clearly perceived by his subordinates and they had no difficulty responding to them.

Once one recognizes several levels of communication, one can open up communication channels that ordinarily are not used. Once the participants in an interpersonal situation obtain some insight into their own communication behavior, they can examine rationally the pros and cons of opening more of the Arrow C, or "confiding," kind of channel. Specifically, they can examine whether or not the effectiveness of the group would be increased if more members shared withheld information or their private feelings relevant to the task at hand, particularly feelings pertaining to other members and to the work situation.

For example, the consultant may face a situation in which

the members of a work group or team will reveal feelings, such as frustration, anger, futility, tenderness, or concern, privately to him, but it never occurs to them to share these feelings with the people who elicit them. The reasons for such withholding are multiple: our culture says it is not polite; it may be hurtful to the other person; there is the danger of angering the other person, leading to retaliation on his part; it may make the relationship too intimate; or it is something that simply does not occur to the person to do.

The consultant can stimulate more open communications by interventions that show the group the price of *not* communicating at this level. The approach would be to start with rather safe topics and areas. A member is against a proposal, but instead of sharing his feeling he starts various political maneuvers to ensure that the proposal will not go through, or, worse, lets it go through and then resists implementing it. If the consultant can get the group to spend some time analyzing its own process, he can raise the question of how members originally felt about the proposal and thus stimulate in a safer environment some opening up of earlier feelings. If this exercise proves illuminating and productive to the group, they are likely to be a bit more open in the next work session, although the consultant has to expect this kind of learning to be very slow and erratic.

Exploration of the B-type communication is most relevant if the group is having serious communication problems. The consultant can then raise the question of whether members are confusing each other by sending more than one message at once, creating for the recipient the problem of which one to react to. It should be noted that if the group agrees to discuss this issue at all, the members must reveal some of their own reactions. In other words, if I tell someone that he is sending a B-type message, thus reducing one of his blind spots, I am at the same time revealing something of my reactions that I ordinarily hide, thus reducing the size of my own concealed areas. Discussions of either B- or C-type messages tend thus to stimulate each other. The desired result would be a situation in which all members could enlarge their own open areas in their dealings with each other, thereby reducing distortions, miscommunications, and ambiguities.

On the other hand, nothing in the PC philosophy argues

for openness as being in and of itself a good thing. It all depends on whether or not relevant information that would make accomplishment of the group's task easier is being withheld. Being more open then would increase group effectiveness, provided being open was culturally permissible. In many cultures there are areas that are interpersonally taboo and cannot be opened up no matter what the cost of withholding. In such instances the consultant would not be helpful if he simply encouraged more openness.

Filtering

The final, and perhaps most difficult, complexity to consider in the communication process is that both the sender and the receiver use a number of filters in selecting what they will send and what they will receive. I am not implying conscious censorship, although this occurs also. Rather, I am implying that all of us select what we say, how we say it, and when we say it in terms of a complex set of decision rules that we have learned over a lifetime and that reflect a number of specific factors:

1. Self-image. Both sender and the receiver have an image or concept of themselves and feelings of self-worth or self-esteem. What their self-concept is at any given time and what value they attach to themselves in a given situation will, in part, determine their communication. For example, if I think of myself as an expert in an area and have great confidence in myself (attach great worth to myself) in a given situation, I am more likely to communicate in the first place, more likely to choose an assertive, telling style of communication rather than a diffident one, and less likely to listen to others on that same topic. After all, I am the expert.

2. Image of the Other Person or Persons. Both the sender and the receiver have an image or concept of the others in the situation and attach certain values to these others as people. These images of the others will also, in part, determine communication. For example, if I see the others in the situation as being less expert and of lower status in the situation than I am, I am likely to talk down to them, to interrupt them when I think they are off target, to listen less for their original points of view and more for whether they are understanding me and/or agreeing with me. If I feel less expert or of lower status I will say less, listen harder, and try to figure out how to gain status in the situation (this, incidentally, may inhibit good listening also, diverting attention from the task to the relationship issue).

3. Definition of the Situation. Both the sender and the receiver have a certain picture of the situation in which they are jointly operating. Is it a meeting to solve a specific problem? Is it an informal bull session? Are we here to give the boss a chance to tell us his ideas? Often this process of "defining the situation" is not verbalized until someone raises the question "What are we here for?" or "What is our task?"

The definition of the situation goes beyond specifying the goals or task to be achieved; it is the complete set of perceptions pertaining to one's own and others' roles in the situation, its duration, its boundaries, and the norms that will govern it (for example, is it a formal or informal situation?). Obviously, what we say and how we say it will be largely governed by how we define the situation.

4. Motives, Feelings, Intentions, Attitudes. Another set of filters on the communication process both for sender and listener are the various needs and motives they bring to the situation, their intentions, and their attitudes toward others. If my needs are to sell a proposal or to influence others, I will communicate differently from how I will if I am curious about something and need to get information. If I am trying to influence, I will listen differently to what others say from how I will if I am gathering information, and I will listen for different things. For example, if I am trying to influence, I will listen harder for agreement or disagreement than for new ideas.

5. Expectations. The final category of psychological factors that create filters is our expectations of ourselves and of others in the situation, based either on actual experience or on preconceptions and stereotypes. If I expect my audience to be slow to understand, I will use simpler words; if I expect them to be receptive, I will talk in a more relaxed way; if I expect them to be critical, I will frame my points carefully and precisely.

From the point of view of the listener, if he expects the speaker to be very smart, he may read in more meaning than there is in the message; if he expects him to be inarticulate or unintelligent, he may fail to hear the good points. If he expects disagreement, he may read hostility into what the speaker says; and if he expects support, he may fail to hear disagreement.

Given all the various filters described, it is not surprising that the communication process between people is fraught with so much difficulty. The process consultant is not immune to the psychological factors described. He will have his own set of filters based upon his needs, expectations, images, intentions, and so on. Because he is a trained observer he may spot the effects of filters sooner than other members, but he certainly cannot see the truth in any absolute sense any better than other members can. It is partly for this reason that he must help the group to make a diagnosis rather than simply providing his own diagnosis as if it were the absolute truth. Only out of the joint efforts of all the members can a diagnosis of communications difficulties be made that is likely to be near enough to the truth to warrant remedial action.

The Circular Process and Self-fulfilling Prophecies

The various factors described above under the category of filtering make it possible for communications to break down in a particularly dangerous manner. If expectations are strong on the part of both the sender and the receiver, it is possible for each to interpret the cues from the other in such a way that both confirm their stereotypes and thus lock each other into roles from which it is difficult to escape. Let us take two examples.

Person A, on the basis of previous experience, has a positive self-image, is confident, needs to influence others, and expects to be able to do so. His communications are assertive, confident, and clear. His listeners respond to this clarity and assertiveness by paying attention to what he has to say, thus confirming A's image of himself as an influential person. He gains confidence from being listened to and assumes an increasingly strong role in the group.

Person B, on the basis of his previous experience, is not sure of himself, feels a lack of confidence in the presence of several others, is not sure he can influence people even though he would like to, and expects that he will have difficulty establishing himself in the group. His communications will, as a result, be hesitant, low key, and diffident, although they may be just as clear as A's.

His listeners may well respond to the diffidence and hesitancy by assuming that B does not have much to offer and may cease to pay attention to him, thus confirming his own initial impression of himself as having little to contribute. B loses confidence, communicates less and less, further confirming for the others his lack of potential contribution, and gradually assumes the role of a noncontributor.

In both cases the final outcome is the result of initial expectations that produce a certain communication style, which in turn leads to confirmation of the initial expectations. The danger is that the initial expectations may have little to do with the actual potential contribution of A and B to the group product; yet A will be a high contributor and B will be a low contributor. Only by becoming sensitive to this kind of self-fulfilling prophecy can the group protect itself from getting a mix of contributions that are unrelated to actual ability.

A key role for the process consultant is to ask himself, when he observes different rates of participation and contribution to the group, whether this accurately reflects ability to contribute or is the result of circular processes of the sort described. If the consultant finds evidence for the latter, he must help the group reassess its own operations, reexamine its stereotypes of who can contribute what, and build norms that permit the low-confidence contributor to gain confidence by being listened to by others.

Summary

In the previous sections I have examined various facets of the communication process. Starting with relatively overt processes, such as who talks, who talks to whom, who interrupts whom, and what style of communication is used, I then reviewed more subtle communication issues, such as the meaning implicit in nonverbal communication, the role of different levels of communication stemming from our blind spots and tendencies to conceal certain things about ourselves, and the problems stemming from our tendencies to filter in the role of both sender and receiver.

This set of issues by no means exhausts all aspects of communication that could be reviewed. For example, we did not cover problems of semantics, nor did we examine issues involving how to communicate in a more persuasive way — subjects one might find in courses on "good" communications. Topics covered reflect those aspects of communication that tend to be especially important in work teams, staff meetings, bull sessions, committees, and other settings where member relations have to be "good" in order for work output to be high. The process consultant must help the group to perceive the connection between the subtle communication processes described and the kind of factual exchange that leads to effective working relations and high output.

4

The Process of Building and Maintaining a Group

One of the most salient phenomena I encounter in the early contacts with a client organization is groups at all stages of development. The clients who come to visit me to explore a possible consultation may not have worked with each other before and thus may be a brand new small group. The committee meeting that I am asked to attend may be a special meeting of a group that has regular meetings every week or, on the other hand, may be a group that has met for the very first time to consider the consulting project. The people that the client may have invited to meet with me may include some who have worked extensively with each other and a few others who are, in effect, strangers to each other at the initial meeting. Given this variety of circumstances, it is essential for the consultant to have a simplifying model of how a group gets started and develops.

The underlying theoretical premise is that when two or more people come together to form a work- or task-oriented group, there will first be a period of essentially self-oriented behavior reflecting various concerns that any new member of a group could be expected to experience. As the self-oriented behavior declines, members begin to pay more attention to each other and to the task at hand. The kinds of behavior that help the group to build and maintain itself then occur concurrently with behaviors designed to accomplish the work of the group. I would like to describe the steps in a chronological sequence because they occur more or less in sequence, although each phase may overlap the others.

Phase 1: Problems in Entering a New Group; Self-oriented Behavior

The problems that a person faces when he enters a new group stem from certain underlying emotional issues that must be resolved before he can feel comfortable in the new situation. Four such issues can be readily identified (see Fig. 4–1).

Problems	*Resulting feelings*	*Coping responses (self-oriented)*
1. *IDENTITY*		1. *"TOUGH" RESPONSES*
Who am I to be?	Frustration	Fighting, controlling resisting authority.
2. *CONTROL & INFLUENCE*		2. *"TENDER" RESPONSES*
Will I be able to control and influence others?	Tension	Supporting, helping forming alliances, dependency.
3. *NEEDS & GOALS*	Anxiety	3. *WITHDRAWAL OR DENIAL RESPONSES*
Will the group goals include my own needs?		Passivity, indifference, overuse of "logic and reason"
4. *ACCEPTANCE & INTIMACY*		
Will I be liked and accepted by the group? How close a group will we be?		

Figure 4–1
Problems in Entering a New Group Which Cause Self-oriented Behavior

1. Identity First and foremost is the problem of choosing a role or identity that will be acceptable to the person himself and viable in the group. In other words, each new member, whether he is aware of it or not, must find an answer to the question "Who and what am I to be in this group?"

This issue exists in the first place because all of us have a large repertory of possible roles and behavioral styles to bring into play in any given situation. Should I be the dominant aggressive leader, a behavior pattern that may have worked for me in some situations; or should I be the humorous tension reliever, which may have worked for me in other situations; or should I be the quiet listener, which has worked in still other situations? In varying degrees we are different people in different life situations. Therefore we always have some degree of choice in new situations.

In formal committees or work groups, this kind of issue is often partially resolved through the initial mandate. A person is told to join a task force to represent the "personnel point of view," or a strong chairman tells members what kinds of roles he wants them to play. Such resolutions are at best only partial, however, in that there is still great latitude for the person to develop a style that will satisfy him and be acceptable to the others in the group. As Figure 4–1 indicates, as long as the emotional issue is there, whether the person recognizes it consciously or not, it operates as a source of tension, leads the person to be primarily preoccupied with himself, and consequently leads to less listening and concern for others or the group task.

2. Control, Power, Influence A second issue that any new member faces and which must be resolved in any new group is the distribution of power and influence. It can be safely assumed that every member will have some need to control and influence others, but the amount of this need and its form of expression will vary from person to person. One member may wish to influence the actual task solution, another may wish to influence the methods or procedures used by the group, a third may wish to achieve an overall position of prominence in the group, and so on.

The dilemma for all members early in the group's history

is that they do not know each other's needs or styles, and hence cannot easily determine who will be able to influence whom and what. Consequently, the consultant will frequently observe a great deal of fencing, testing each other out, and experimenting with different forms of influence in early meetings. The consultant must be careful not to misunderstand this behavior. On the surface it seems like a definite flight from whatever task the group is facing. Underneath it represents an important sorting out, getting acquainted, and coming to terms with each other which the members need to do in order to relax their self-concerns and focus on the task.

If a chairman insists on a tight formal schedule that prevents some of this getting acquainted and testing out, he runs the risk of either producing superficial solutions because members are not ready to really work on the task, or of forcing them to do their fencing in the context of the task work, thereby slowing down the progress and undermining the potential quality of the solution. In this kind of situation, the consultant must help the chairman to understand the functions the initial sorting-out behavior performs for the members, to understand the need for group building time, and to understand that good communications cannot develop until members' self-preoccupations have been reduced.

3. *Individual Needs and Group Goals* A third issue that faces every group member is his concern that the group goals that are initially set or will emerge from discussion may not include his personal goals and needs. Preoccupation with this issue typically leads the person to wait and see how the group develops, not to invest himself too heavily in it until he sees whether things will go his way. The problem for the group as a whole is that if a substantial number of people take the wait-and-see attitude, it is difficult to get any group action started. In this situation the group typically turns to any available authority to set the agenda, formulate goals, or suggest a task. If the chairman responds to the pressure and sets the goals, he is partially solving the problem, but he still cannot ensure that the goals he sets will involve all the members sufficiently to get them committed to the task.

A sounder procedure would be to face the paradox directly: *Until member needs are to some degree exposed and shared, it is not possible to set up valid group goals.* Consequently, enough meeting time should be allocated to permit members to explore what they really want to get out of the group. The role of the process consultant in this situation is usually to slow down the group and to reassure members that the early struggles to communicate with each other are a necessary and important part of group growth.

4. *Acceptance and Intimacy* These two issues are lumped together because they deal with the same underlying problem: Will I be liked and accepted by the others in the group, and how close or intimate will we have to be to achieve a comfortable level of mutual respect and acceptance? For every set of people and every situation, norms must be developed by the group that help to resolve these issues. There is no optimal or absolute level of acceptance and intimacy for all groups at all times. It depends on the members, on the group task, on the length of time available to the group, and a host of other factors. But the issue is always there as a source of tension until working norms have been established.

Initially the issue will appear in terms of forms of address and patterns of politeness. As the group develops, the issue will center on formality or informality of group procedures. At a still later stage the issue will center on whether group discussion must stick to the formal task or whether more personal exchanges are permissible and desirable.

The group can attempt to legislate solutions by the adoption of Roberts's Rules of Order or similar devices, but such procedures are more likely to sweep the issue under the rug than really to resolve it. The role of the consultant can be to help the group to recognize that the issue is a legitimate one to be worked on.

Types of Coping Responses to Emotional Issues

As indicated above, each of the underlying problems in gaining membership leads to tension, frustration, and self-preoccupation. What does the person typically do in coping with the underlying problems and the resulting tensions? Three basic kinds of coping patterns can be observed (see Fig. 4–1):

1. Basically tough, aggressive coping
2. Basically tender, support-seeking coping
3. Coping by withdrawal behavior based on denial of any feelings

The *tough, aggressive response* shows up in various kinds of fighting, such as arguing, cutting down other members' points, ridiculing, deliberate ignoring of others, cutting and hostile humor, and the like. Although the behavior may be legitimate within the rules of group discussion under the guise of "debating the point" or "exploring our differences," the observer should be careful to note whether the underlying feelings expressed are concern for a better task solution or are, in fact, ways of challenging and testing other members in the process of solving emotional issues.

The aggressive response also is reflected in attempts to control other members through setting up procedures, calling on people, telling other members what they should be talking about, and the like. With respect to any authority figures in the group, such as the chairman, this type of emotional behavior shows up as counterdependency. Counterdependency refers to feelings of wanting to resist authority: "Let's find out what the chairman wants us to do and then *not* do it," or "Let's do it our own way, not the way he wants us to do it."

In most formal groups such behavior is likely to be quite subtle because standards of politeness and formal power differences militate against open expressions of counterdependency. Yet it is not difficult for the process consultant to observe such behavior, to help the group to recognize the legitimacy of it, and to help differentiate emotional coping from genuine expression of differences on the task level.

The *tender, support-seeking response* is reflected in a variety of ways. Members look for someone with whom they seem to agree and try to form a supportive alliance or subgroup within the larger group. Members attempt to avoid conflict, give support, help each other, and generally try to suppress aggressive, divisive feelings. With respect to authority, such behavior shows up as dependency — looking for someone to lean on, to give guidance, and to solve the problems that the members feel they have.

How does the process consultant differentiate this kind of behavior from constructive problem-solving behavior? First, he notes at what point in the group's or member's history the behavior is occurring. As I have indicated, the emotionally based self-oriented behavior occurs early in the history when members are trying to establish themselves in the group. The same kind of behavior later could simply mean genuine support in reference to the task.

A second criterion is whether the consultant feels that the support is based on genuine mutual understanding or is a kind of blind response. The emotionally based behavior I am describing here is often indicated by members forming alliances without really showing evidence of understanding each other's points of view at all. The consultant must help the group to distinguish hasty support seeking, indiscriminate helping, and inappropriate dependency from similar behaviors that may occur later in the process of problem solving.

The *withdrawal or denial response* is characterized by a suppression of tension and feeling, often resulting in a rather passive, indifferent, bland kind of response. It is as if the person were saying, "You people go ahead and fight it out and get this group rolling while I watch; I don't really have any feelings about it, so I'll get on board when things get properly organized."

Another version of this emotional behavior is for the person to argue that feelings have no place in group discussion and should be legislated out of existence and suppressed at all costs. When a fight breaks out, the person says, "Fellow members, we are all civilized, mature individuals; we can settle this logically and calmly. Let us not let our feelings get the better of us; let's stick to the facts."

If the person were being truly rational and logical, he would realize that the feelings in the situation are some of the facts that must be taken into account. They can be suppressed and legislated off the agenda, but they cannot be made to disappear and they cannot be prevented from affecting each member's problem-solving behavior. If a group member has tensions and self-preoccupations, he will in fact not be listening to or concerned about other members and hence will not contribute to effective problem solving.

Each of us, as a human being, is capable of each of these basic types of response in our efforts to cope with the emotional issues of the group. Which style of response we tend to use will depend on our personalities, on our past histories in interpersonal situations, on the behavior of other members in the group, and on the formality and structure of the situation. For example, a formal, tightly controlled group is much more likely to produce withdrawal and denial responses, which in the long run will produce a poorly motivated, alienated group. When such a group tries to solve a difficult problem, there is no guarantee that members will either be motivated enough to direct their energies to the problem or be able to communicate with each other well enough to build a genuine group solution. Permitting and exploring emotional expressions, on the other hand, will lead to initial discomfort but will, in the long run, produce a higher level of communication and a stronger, more effective group.

Resolution of Emotional Issues

I have described four kinds of emotional issues that every person faces when he enters a new group situation — the problem of identity, the problem of influence and power, the problem of needs and goals, and the problem of acceptance and intimacy. Until the person finds a role for himself in the group and until the group develops norms pertaining to goals, influence, and intimacy, he will be tense and will respond in various emotional ways.

The price of such behavior for the group is that the members are preoccupied with their own feelings and hence less able to listen to each other and solve problems. Yet every group must go through some growing pains while members work on these issues and find their place. If the formal structure does not permit such growth, the group never becomes a real group capable of group effort. It remains a collection of individuals held together by a formal structure.

The process consultant can help the group to resolve emotional issues in a number of ways. First of all, he must be aware of what is going on and not become anxious over the initial communication problems that members have. Second, he must help the group to realize that the early fighting, alliances, and withdrawal responses are efforts on the part of members to get to know each other, to test each other out, and to find their own place in the group. He can do this by giving the group perspective on itself through capsules of group theory of the sort I have given here. He can indicate his belief that members are working on a legitimate group-building task, not just wasting time.

In order to be helpful, the consultant must fully understand how groups form and which issues are involved in the evolution of group norms and eventually a group culture (Schein, 1985). In particular he must be aware that, as individual self-oriented behavior declines and the group begins to take shape, it must manage both its external relations and its internal functioning in order to survive and function well.

Process management takes insight, time, and energy. I find myself, as a process consultant, having to help managers accept the reality of the investments they must make in group functioning. Managers typically expect groups to be able to get right to work and do not allow for a period of group building. If the group does not solve problems quickly, members get angry and disillusioned with group effort. The consultant must then encourage managers to be patient, to allocate enough time to group meetings to permit the group to grow, and to realize that their own anger and impatience are a reflection of the same emotional issues that the other members are facing.

Finally, the consultant must be expert in giving helpful and useful feedback to members concerning their own behavior. Much of the coping is likely to be occurring without awareness on the part of the group members as to what is happening and why. If they are to gain some insight into this behavior and become more expert in diagnosing it themselves, the consultant must try to help each member to understand his own coping behavior.

As members acquire this insight, as they begin to know how others are feeling and responding, and as they begin to realize that the group can include them and their potential contribution, they gradually relax and their ability to pay attention to others increases. When this happens one can sense a change in the climate and mood of the group. There is less urgency, more listening, less running away from tasks to be performed, more willingness to cooperate as a total group, less formality and falling back on arbitrary rules, but more self-discipline and willingness to suppress personal agendas for the sake of the total group performance. The important thing to realize is that such a state can be achieved only if the group is permitted to work out its internal and external problems. It cannot be imposed or legislated.

Phase 2: Task and Group-Maintenance Functions

So far I have discussed what happens in the early life of a group before it is ready to solve problems effectively. In the following sections I will deal with various aspects of group problem solving and the contributions that members make to it. Figure 4–2 shows a list of what have been called *task* functions and *maintenance* functions. These are behaviors that must occur to some degree inside the group in order for the group to progress effectively. The group must also maintain itself in its environment and fulfill *boundary maintenance* functions.

From the point of view of the process consultant, the lists are important as a checking device to determine which kinds of functions are being performed adequately and which are either missing altogether or not adequately performed. The observer of process can also study the distribution of the functions to determine whether they are evenly distributed, whether some members consistently do one kind of thing, which functions the leader performs, and so on.

A. Task Functions

Let us look at some task functions first. In order for the group to make progress on a task, there must be some *initiating*. Someone must state the goal or problem, make proposals as to how to work on it, set some time limits or targets, and the like. Often this function falls to the leader or to whoever called the

Task Functions	*Building and Maintenance Functions*
Initiating	Harmonizing
Information seeking	Compromising
Information giving	Gatekeeping
Opinion seeking	Encouraging
Opinion giving	Diagnosing
Clarifying	Standard setting
Elaborating	Standard testing
Summarizing	
Consensus testing	

Boundary Management Functions

Boundary defining
Scouting
Negotiating
Translating
Guarding
Managing entry and exit

Figure 4–2
Task, Building, and Maintenance Functions in Groups

group together in the first place, but as a group grows and gains confidence, initiating functions will increasingly come from a broader range of members.

In order for progress to be made there must be some *opinion seeking and giving* and *information seeking and giving* on various issues related to the task. The kinds of information and opinions a group seeks in pursuing its tasks are often crucial for the quality of the solution. The observer should note carefully and help the group to observe for itself whether sufficient time was given to the information- and opinion-seeking functions. It is also important to distinguish seeking from giving and information from opinion. Groups often have difficulty because too many members give opinions before sufficient information seeking and giving has occurred, leading then to fruitless debate. The consultant can help by asking what kinds of information might be needed to resolve the issue among different opinions that are on the floor.

Clarifying and *elaborating* are critical functions in a group in order to test the adequacy of communication and in order to build on the ideas of others toward more creative and complex ideas. If such activities do not occur, the group is not really using its unique strength. One of the most common and powerful interventions that the process consultant can make is to ask clarifying questions or test his own listening by elaborating some of the ideas of members.

Summarizing is an important function to ensure that ideas are not lost because of either the size of the group or the length of time of discussion. Effective summarizing will include a review of which points the group has already covered and the different ideas that have been stated, so that as decision points are reached, the group is operating with full information. One common problem I have observed in committees, task forces, and executive teams is that they tend to work sequentially and process one idea at a time, never gaining any perspective on the totality of their discussion. What is missing is the summarizing function. It can be fulfilled by having a recorder note ideas on a blackboard as the group proceeds so that it has its own visible summary before it at all times; or a person can, from time to time, simply review what he has heard and draw out tentative generalizations from it for the group to consider. This, along with clarifying, is a most useful function for the consultant.

Finally, the group needs someone periodically to test whether it is nearing a decision or should continue to discuss. *Consensus testing* could involve simply asking the question "Are we ready to decide?" or could involve some summarizing: "It seems to me we have expressed these three alternatives and are leaning toward number two; am I right?" The success of this function in moving the group forward will depend largely on the sensitivity of the person in choosing the right time to test, although ill-timed tests are still useful in reminding the group that it has some more discussing to do.

Task functions such as these are so obviously relevant to

effective group problem solving that it is easy for the process consultant to get the group thinking of process in terms of them. One of the consultant's greatest problems is choosing which behavior to bring to the group's attention. The task functions provide one simple alternative that is not too likely to be resisted as irrelevant.

B. Building and Internal Maintenance Functions

In order for the group to survive and grow as an effective instrument of problem solving, members must concern themselves with the building and maintenance of good relationships. Ideally such concerns would be expressed throughout the life cycle of the group, but, as we have already seen when examining the early phases of group life, members do become preoccupied with their own needs and thus may damage their relationships to others.

The problem for the group is how to rebuild damaged relationships and/or minimize initial tendencies for them to become damaged. By a damaged relationship I mean, for example, two members who are angry at each other because they have opposing views on a task issue, members who were outvoted or ignored and thus feel left out, members who feel misunderstood or sidetracked, and so on. In each case, the person is temporarily preoccupied with personal needs and feelings, and is therefore relatively less able to contribute to group effort. If no group maintenance occurs, the member is not brought back into harmony with the group and is consequently lost as a resource to the group or, worse, becomes an active saboteur of group effort.

Some member activities can best be thought of as preventive maintenance. For example, the function of *gatekeeping* ensures that members who have a contribution to make to problem solution have an opportunity to make it. Gatekeeping thus involves both reducing the activity of overactive members and increasing the activity of overly passive members. I have often sat in a group and observed one person repeatedly open his mouth and actually get one or two words out when a more aggressive person interrupts him, takes the floor away, and make his own point. After two or three attempts, the person gives up, unless someone notices the problem and provides an opportunity for the person to get his point in.

Encouraging may serve a similar function in helping a person to make his point, partly to give the group the benefit of the content, but also to ensure that he and others will feel that the group climate is one of acceptance.

Harmonizing and *compromising* are deliberately placed on the maintenance function list rather than the task function list because they are useful in reducing destructive types of disagreement between individuals, but are definitely of limited usefulness in solving task problems. This is a crucial point because process consultants, in being concerned about group effectiveness, are likely to be seen as favoring harmony and smooth group functioning at all times. In fact, it may be quite necessary for the group to confront and work through tough disagreements to some genuine integrative solution that does not involve any compromising or harmonizing. The consultant may often have to help the group to confront and work through a problem when it would rather back off and compromise. However, if communication has broken down and several members are arguing or taking positions for such self-oriented reasons as maintaining their own status in the group, it may be necessary as a maintenance step to harmonize the conflict and help each member to take stock of his own behavior as a way of reestablishing good communication.

Diagnosing, standard setting, and standard testing are most relevant as remedial measures when relationships have to some degree broken down. What the group then needs is some period of suspending task operations while it (1) looks at its process, checks out how people are feeling about the group, its norms, and its method of operating; and (2) airs the problems and conflicts that may have arisen. Most groups do not engage in this kind of behavior unless a consultant is present or one of the members takes a real process orientation. Yet such periods of reassessment and catharsis are absolutely necessary for most task groups if they are to remain effective.

C. Boundary Management Functions

Every group exists in some kind of organizational or social environment; one of its primary tasks, therefore, is to manage its relationship to that environment (Ancona, 1988).[1]

Boundary defining by specifying who is in and who is not in the group is one of the most fundamental of these functions, and the consultant will observe a variety of behaviors that serve to communicate both to insiders and to outsiders who the group is — special uniforms, styles of communication, names that groups give themselves, minutes of meetings that communicate who is in and who is out through the distribution of who gets them, and so on.

Scouting refers to activities that provide the group the information it needs about its environment. Such information may refer to what is going on so that the group can forecast its own future, which resources are available, what key people in the environment think of the group, which sources of support and sources of danger exist, and so on. The process consultant, himself in a boundary-spanning role, can be especially helpful in identifying when some of the critical scouting functions are not being performed, thus putting the group into jeopardy from unanticipated environmental events.

Negotiating with the environment involves a whole host of activities designed to ensure that the group gets what it needs, manages sources of opportunity or threat, and generally maintains good relations with those people in the environment who can affect the fate of the group. Thus the group will from time to time send out information and appoint ambassadors to negotiate with key outsiders if conflicts of interest are involved or to open up communication channels to other groups as these become necessary.

Translating refers to all those functions involved in figuring out what others' messages mean to the group and in formulating its own messages to the outside in terms that others will understand. In this process of information exchange with the

---

[1]Much less work has been done on defining boundary maintenance functions than on defining internal maintenance functions. The particular ones identified here are based on extensive work by Ancona (1988).

environment, the group will need to filter, classify, and elaborate information to ensure internal comprehension and external acceptance. Here the consultant again has a special opportunity to raise questions about what different words will mean to others as he listens to the group.

An especially important activity in this arena is *technological gatekeeping*, the activity of bringing to the group whatever special information it needs to perform its task (Allen, 1977). In technically oriented groups, such as product development teams in engineering, some members scan the external technical environment to bring to the group those critical information items that bear on their particular task.

Guarding or *patrolling the border* refers to the activities that ensure that the group's sense of integrity will not be violated. Who is invited to meetings, what information is shared with which outsiders, what agreements are made among members about keeping information confidential, how unwelcome visitors are managed, how members are dealt with who leak information or embarrass the group, and so on are among the activities here.

Entry and exit management refers to the processes the group uses to bring in new members (immigrants) and to release present members who leave (emigrants or outcasts). Thus socialization activities, indoctrination, training, and rites of entry would occur around new members, and various kinds of exit rites would be involved for departing members depending on the conditions under which they are leaving. Do members leave because they have been promoted out of the group, because they have been sent on a mission by the group, because they do not like the group, because they do not fit into the group, or because they have violated group norms and are being excommunicated?

Other functions can be identified, and the particular lists I have provided are not necessarily the best ways to classify the various activities and roles that members of a group fulfill. The important point for the process consultant is to recognize that every group must manage its own creation and its own maintenance both internally and externally. By observing how the group manages these various activities and which ones get over- or undermanaged, the consultant can formulate in his mind where interventions are most necessary.

The two phases I have focused on do not describe the entire life cycle of a group (Schein, 1985). As the group matures and develops a culture, it also develops new issues and problems, but these are typically beyond the scope of the consultant's involvement unless he is called to help a group that is stagnating and needs revitalization.

Helping the Group to Learn

How can the process consultant encourage the performance of these kinds of functions on a regular basis? One of the simplest techniques is to suggest that at the end of every meeting (or on some periodic basis) the group allocate some small period of time, such as fifteen to thirty minutes, to review its own meeting and to collect member feelings about how the meeting has gone. Such feelings can be collected in an open-ended way or with the help of such diagnostic instruments as that shown in Figure 4–3. This particular set of questions focuses on internal relationships, but it would be equally appropriate to create a set of questions around external boundary management if the consultant felt that the group needed help in that area.

If a diagnostic questionnaire is used, somewhat more time must be allocated to analysis. If the group is skeptical of the value of any diagnosis, it is better to start with short periods of open-ended discussion, keeping the questionnaire in reserve until the group learns the value of such discussions and is willing to allocate more time to them. The consultant can always start the discussion by focusing on only one or two of the questions where he feels particular issues may have arisen.

The role of the consultant during diagnostic periods must be carefully managed. The great temptation is to rush in, once the group has opened the door, and report all the meaty observations that the consultant has made over the past several hours. This temptation is often heightened by the group's actually inviting the consultant to tell the group all of his observations. "How do you feel we did during the meeting?" "You've been sitting observing us for a couple of hours; what thoughts do you have?"

The consultant must at this time remind himself of his basic mission: to get the group to *share* in diagnosis and to help the group to *learn* to diagnose its own processes. If he succumbs

Rating Group Effectiveness

A: Goals

<u>Poor</u>	1	2	3	4	5	6	7	8	9	10	<u>Good</u>

Confused; diverse; conflicting; indifferent; little interest.

Clear to all; shared by all; all care about the goals, feel involved.

B: Participation

<u>Poor</u>	1	2	3	4	5	6	7	8	9	10	<u>Good</u>

Few dominate; some passive; some not listened to; several talk at once or interrupt.

All get in; all are really listened to.

C: Feelings

<u>Poor</u>	1	2	3	4	5	6	7	8	9	10	<u>Good</u>

Unexpected; ignored or criticized.

Freely expressed; empathic responses.

D: Diagnosis of group problems

<u>Poor</u>	1	2	3	4	5	6	7	8	9	10	<u>Good</u>

Jump directly to remedial proposals; treat symptoms rather than basic causes.

When problems arise the situation is carefully diagnosed before action is proposed; remedies attack basic causes.

(continued)

Figure 4–3
Sample Form for Analyzing Group Effectiveness

E: Leadership

Poor	1	2	3	4	5	6	7	8	9	10	Good

Group needs for leadership not met; group depends too much on single person or on a few persons.

As needs for leadership arise various members meet them ("distributed leadership"); anyone feels free to volunteer as he sees a group need.

F: Decisions

Poor	1	2	3	4	5	6	7	8	9	10	Good

Needed decisions don't get made; decision made by part of group; others uncommitted.

Consensus sought and tested; deviates appreciated and used to improve decision; decisions when made are fully supported.

G: Trust

Poor	1	2	3	4	5	6	7	8	9	10	Good

Members distrust one another; are polite, careful, closed, guarded; they listen superficially but inwardly reject what others say; are afraid to criticize or to be criticized.

Members trust one another; they reveal to group what they would be reluctant to expose to others; they respect and use the responses they get; they can freely express negative reactions without fearing reprisal.

H: Creativity and growth

Poor	1	2	3	4	5	6	7	8	9	10	Good

Members and group in a rut; operate routinely; persons stereotyped and rigid in their roles; no progress.

Group flexible, seeks new and better ways; individuals changing and growing; creative; individually supported.

Figure 4–3 (*Continued*)

and takes the lead in making observations, there is great danger that the group will abdicate its own responsibility for diagnosis. Furthermore, if the consultant makes observations with which some members disagree, he quickly finds himself in a position of having been neutralized. Finally, if the consultant comes in with his own observations first, he is forgetting that his own filters are operating and that he may be reporting things that are relatively less important or which are a reflection of his own biases.

Given these pitfalls, it is important that the process consultant encourage the group not only to allocate time for diagnosis but to take the lead itself in trying to articulate and understand its own processes. Once the group has identified an area where members themselves have observations to make, it is entirely appropriate for the consultant to add his own observations and to use the opportunity to deepen members' understanding by offering not only observations but some group theory. But the group must take the lead, and the consultant must work within the areas defined by the group as relevant. If the group urges the consultant to do this job *for them*, he must politely decline and urge the group in turn to try its own hand at diagnosis.

Summary

Thus far we have been focusing on various aspects and functions of the individual's behavior in the group. We have examined the causes of self-oriented behavior and types of self-oriented behavior. We then examined various task functions relevant to getting a job done, and various maintenance functions relevant to keeping the group in good working order and managing the group's relationship with its external environment. Having dealt with these basics, let us proceed to an analysis of the processes involved in the actual work of the group: problem solving and decision making.

5

Group Problem Solving and Decision Making

Groups in organizations generally exist for a purpose. They have a function or are supposed to work on a task or to solve a problem. Whether we are focusing on a two-person group, such as a client and I trying to establish a relationship, or a task force meeting that I have been asked to attend as part of getting acquainted with the client organization, there is always a task explicitly or implicitly defined, there are always problems to be solved, decisions to be made, and time and effort to be managed. How does a group tackle and solve problems?

Problem Solving

Problem solving as a process is much discussed and little understood. I propose to give the reader not an ultimately valid model of this process but a practical model that is amenable to observation and analysis. The steps or stages I will describe and analyze are applicable to any kind of problem-solving process, whether it occurs in an individual manager's head, in a two-person group, in a large committee, or in the total organization. My focus will remain, as in past chapters, on the small group because it is in this size unit that the process consultant is often most likely to be able to make his contribution.

The basic model as presented in Figure 5–1 is an elaboration of a model originally developed by Richard Wallen for use in sensitivity training programs. It distinguishes two basic cycles of activity — one that occurs prior to any decision or action, and one that occurs after a decision to act has been taken. The first cycle consists of three stages:

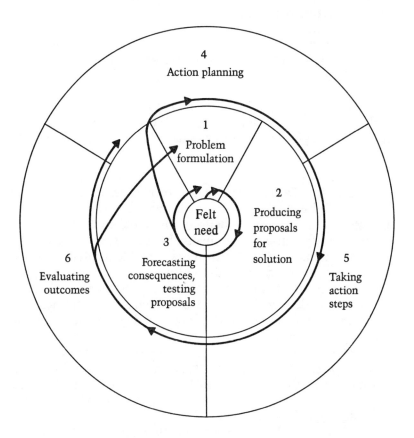

Figure 5–1
A Model of the Stages of Problem Solving

1. Problem formulation
2. Generating proposals for action
3. Forecasting consequences of proposed solutions or testing proposed solutions and evaluating them conceptually before committing to final action.

This cycle ends when the group has made a formal decision on what to do. The second cycle then involves the following:

4. Action planning
5. Action steps
6. Evaluation of the outcomes of the action steps, often leading back to the first cycle with problem redefinition.

The basic reason for breaking the total process into stages such as these is that when problem solving goes awry, it is generally because a given stage is mismanaged or is missing altogether.

Cycle 1

Problem Formulation In my own experience in solving problems and watching others solve them, by far the most difficult step is the first one — defining the problem. The difficulty arises in part because of a confusion between *symptoms* and the *problem*. A manager typically starts a problem-solving process when someone brings some difficulty to his attention or he discovers something that is not as it should be. Sales have fallen off, a schedule for delivery has not been met, an angry customer is on the phone, the production line has broken down, there is a fire in the shop, or whatever.

None of the things mentioned are really "the problem" to be worked on, however. Rather, they are the symptoms to be removed. Before the manager can begin to solve the problem he must identify or find it, and this is the crucial and often most difficult stage of the whole cycle.

Let us take the example of sales falling off, to illustrate the complexity. Manager X has called together his key subordinates and they sit down to discuss "the problem" of declining sales. If the manager is not sensitive to the issue raised above, he may soon be in the midst of a discussion of whether the advertising budget should be raised or ten more men should be sent into the field. But has he as yet defined his problem? Has he even identified what the various alternative problems might be that could cause a reduction in sales?

Falling sales could have any number of causes — erroneous sales forecast (which implies doing nothing out in the field but something in the marketing department), a competitor entering the market suddenly, a drop in product quality, loss of two key salesmen to a competitor, a change in consumer taste, and so on. Without some preliminary diagnosis — which, incidentally, may take time and effort — the manager won't know what is really causing the discrepancy between forecast and actual sales. He won't know what he should really be working on.

The process consultant can often play a key role at this stage because he is less likely to react to the time pressure the manager is under, and therefore is more likely to notice premature shortcuts in reasoning and misdiagnoses. His role is often to help the group to slow down and recognize that it may be acting hastily on an ill-defined problem, and that some initial time invested in identifying what is really the problem will pay off in less wasted time and effort later.

A special category of problems deserves particular mention in this regard — those involving interpersonal relations. A manager says he has a "problem" in motivating a subordinate, or coordinating with another department, or influencing his boss, or integrating the efforts of several people. Often these "problems" are felt as frustrations and tensions, with a minimum of clear understanding on the part of the manager of what is actually frustrating him or making him tense. In a sense he knows something is not right, but he does not know what the problem really is.

In instances such as these, the process consultant can help the manager or the group to identify its problem by asking them to identify concrete incidents or examples of events that led to their feelings of frustration. By carefully going over these incidents in detail and trying to identify which event actually triggered the frustration, one can often define the real problem. The essential step is to examine the concrete incidents and to generalize the problem from these.

This process, as shown in Figure 5–2, is a necessary step in any problem formulation and is the one most often skipped, leading to premature closure on what may be an incorrect diagnosis of the problem. In the falling sales example, the group should carefully reconstruct when and where exactly all the instances of falling sales have occurred, and then determine what those instances have in common.

Producing Proposals for Solution Once the problem has been adequately formulated, the group can move on to producing ideas or courses of action that might resolve the problem. At this stage the most likely pitfall is that proposals are evaluated one at a time. Thus the group is never permitted to gain perspective on the problem by looking at a whole array of possible ideas for solution.

The process consultant can help here by pointing out the consequences of premature evaluations: (1) there is insufficient opportunity for ideas to be judged in perspective because they cannot be compared to other ideas, and (2) the evaluation tends to threaten not only a given idea but the person who proposed it. Members whose ideas have been rejected early may feel less inclined to offer ideas at a later stage.

The group should be encouraged to start this stage with some version of brainstorming — producing a number of ideas and keeping them all in front of the group before any of them are evaluated as such. Brainstorming is built on the rule that no evaluation of ideas should be permitted during the idea-production phase to stimulate the creativity that is needed at this point.

Figure 5–2
Necessary Steps in Initially Formulating the Problem

Once a number of ideas have been laid out, the group can weed out the obviously unworkable ones and go to the next stage with the two or three ideas for problem solution that look like they might work.

Forecasting Consequences and Testing Solutions The next stage of testing ideas by forecasting the consequences of any given solution and evaluating those consequences is often a difficult one because the criteria the group should be using to do its evaluating are not clear. Testing criteria include (1) personal experience, (2) expert opinion, (3) surveying of existing data or information, and/or (4) planned scientific tests or research.

Personal experience and expert opinion are the easiest to obtain but the least valid. Surveys and research are more valid but also more time consuming and expensive. One of the key functions of the process consultant at this stage is to provide to the group this range of alternatives, to enable it to correctly match its validation method to the kind of idea it is trying to test. For example, if the group is trying to decide between two products to develop, it should probably do some market research and test marketing; if the group is trying to decide whether to put surplus funds into capital expansion or investment programs, it should obtain advice from financial experts; and so on. All too often a group uses just one validation method, no matter what ideas are being evaluated.

At each stage of problem solving the discussion may reveal new features that lead to a reformulation of the problem. For example, in testing the idea that a new advertising campaign is needed, examining existing information may reveal that the advertising campaign was perfectly sound. This discovery then raises the question whether the initial formulation of the problem as "consumer sales resistance" was correct. The consultant should help the group to recognize that this kind of recycling, from initial formulation through idea production and idea testing to reformulation of the problem, is a very sound way to solve the problem. Reassurance from the consultant is usually necessary until a group becomes experienced in sensing its own problem-solving cycle because of the tendency to believe that constant reformulation of the problem is merely wasting time.

Cycle 2

All of cycle 1 involves steps that occur in discussion and that do not involve commitment to action unless the group chooses to gather some additional data for idea evaluation. As the group reaches some consensus on a proposed solution and makes a decision to act, we go into cycle 2, or the action cycle. The making of the decision is not shown in the diagram but is represented by the act of crossing the boundary between cycle 1 and cycle 2.

Although a decision has been made on a given proposal or idea for solution, the problem-solving process is far from finished. The group must then still plan a detailed course of action, take action steps, and provide for some method to determine whether or not the action steps are solving the problem. This last step should be thought out in advance: "What information should we be looking at to determine whether or not our action steps are achieving the desired results?"

At any of these stages, it is again possible for the group to discover that it had not formulated the problem correctly; hence it may revert back to cycle 1 for some new reformulation and idea proposing and testing. Again I want to emphasize that such recycling is entirely desirable and should not be considered a waste of time. It is far more costly to be working on the wrong problem, and discover this only after expensive action steps have been taken, than to make an initially greater effort to define the problem correctly. Yet, as a process consultant I have found it difficult to get groups to go back to step 1 and ask themselves the questions: "Have we formulated the problem correctly? Are we working on the right thing?"

Action Planning and Implementation The stage of action planning can be treated as a new problem requiring its own problem formulation stage (What is the problem in implementing the proposal we have decided on?), idea production (What are some alternative ways of implementing this proposal?), and idea testing (Which of our alternatives is the best way to implement this proposal?).

If these substages are short-circuited or avoided, a good proposal may be carried out inadequately and the group will erroneously conclude that the proposal was deficient instead of recognizing insufficient action planning as the culprit. Here again, the key role for the consultant may be to slow the group down and encourage it to plan carefully before leaping into action.

One of the major pitfalls of this stage is to make general plans without assigning clear responsibilities for who is to implement what. I have sat in many a group meeting where a decision was reached, the meeting was adjourned, and nothing happened because everyone thought that someone else would now do something. The clear allocation of responsibility for action not only ensures that action will be taken but provides a test of the decision in that the responsible implementer may raise questions about the decision that had not been considered before.

In some cases the whole second cycle is delegated to some other person or group. For example, the original problem-solving group decides "Let's beef up our advertising campaign." Once it has reached this decision, the group orders the advertising department to increase advertising on certain products. The group then relaxes and reverts to watching sales figures. Is this a sound approach? The answer in many cases is "No."

The major problem, when different people or groups perform cycle 1 and cycle 2, is that the second person (or group) may neither understand clearly nor be particularly committed to the proposal or solution that the cycle 1 person (or group) has offered. He has not struggled with the problem definition; he has not had a chance to see the reasons why other alternatives that may now occur to him have been rejected; and he may not feel that the general proposal given to him is clear enough to permit implementation.

Equally problematic is the case where a group delegates cycle 1 to a task force or a consulting organization and then waits for a proposal in writing. In nine cases out of ten, if the originating group has not involved itself in cycle 1 and if the task force has not thought through cycle 2, the group will not like the proposal and will find an excuse to shelve it.

Given these kinds of problems, it is desirable to ensure a high degree of communication between cycle 1 and cycle 2 persons or groups. The ideal situation would, of course, be that they are the same problem-solving unit. If that is not possible, the cycle 1 unit should provide for an interim phase that permits the cycle 2 unit to get completely on board before the two units sever their communication link.

One way to do this is to bring the implementer into the problem-solving process at the earliest possible stage, or, at least, review completely with the implementer all the steps the cycle 1 unit has gone through in its efforts to arrive at a proposal for solution. In such a review, the key process would be to permit the implementer to satisfy himself completely by asking as many questions as he would like concerning the reasons that certain other alternatives, which might strike him as better ones, were not selected. Either he should get satisfactory answers, or the cycle 1 group should go back and review the additional alternatives brought up by the implementer.

A good problem-solving group will protect itself against communication breakdown at the implementation stage by consulting the implementers at the earliest stages of idea production. If all their ideas are inserted early, there is less likelihood of missing important alternatives, and less likelihood of choosing something that will not make any sense to, or may be misunderstood by, the implementer. The role of the process consultant here is to help the group understand how difficult it is to communicate a complex solution to an implementer, and to ensure this understanding early enough in the problem-solving process to institute protective measures against communication breakdown. And there is no better protective method than to involve the ultimate implementer in the problem solving at the earliest possible stage.

Evaluating Outcomes To ensure adequate evaluation, the group should reach consensus on (1) the criteria that will be used for evaluation, (2) the timetable — when results should first be expected, and (3) who will be responsible for reporting back information to be evaluated.

The other critical point about this stage is that one should be psychologically prepared to go back into cycle 1 with an effort to reformulate the problem, not merely to rush in with more effort or a new solution. A good problem formulation is three-quarters of the solution, so the group should always be prepared to reconsider what it sees the problem to be, and the consultant should constantly raise the question "What problem are we working on?"

The purpose of presenting the problem-solving process as a series of cycles rather than a linear progression is to highlight the importance of going back to earlier stages as new information is revealed.

Group Decision Making

One of the key steps in the problem-solving process is the making of decisions. Decisions are involved at every stage of the process but are only highly visible in the transition from cycle 1 to cycle 2, where the problem-solving unit commits itself to trying out a proposal for action. Prior to this step the group has had to decide when and where to meet, how to organize itself, how to allocate time, by what procedures or rules to run its discussion (for example, with or without a formal chairman, with or without Roberts's Rules of Order), how to tell when the problem has been sufficiently well formulated to move on to idea production, and so on. Often group members do not recognize that they have made so many process decisions and that these have real consequences for the climate of the group and the quality of problem solutions. The consultant must be prepared, therefore, to draw attention to the many mechanisms by which groups make decisions.

In reviewing the different decision-making methods listed below, it is important that we do not quickly judge any one method as better than another. Each has its use at the appropriate time, and each method has certain consequences for future group operations. The important point is for the group to understand these consequences well enough to be able to choose a decision-making method that will be appropriate to the amount of time available, the past history of the group, the kind of task being worked on, and the kind of climate the group wants to establish.

1. Decision by Lack of Response ("Plop") The most common and perhaps least visible group decision-making method occurs when someone suggests an idea, and, before anyone else has said anything about it, someone else suggests another idea, until the group finds one it will act on. All the ideas that have been bypassed have, in a real sense, been decided on by the group. But the decision has been simply a common decision *not* to support them, making the proposers feel that their suggestions have "plopped." The floors of most group meeting rooms are completely covered with plops.

2. Decision by Formal Authority or Self-authorization Many groups set up a power structure or start with a power structure that makes clear the fact that the chairman or someone in authority will make the decisions. The group can generate ideas and hold free discussion, but at any time the chairman can say that, having heard the discussion, he has decided to do thus and so. This method is highly efficient. Whether it is effective depends a great deal on whether the chairman is a sufficiently good listener to have culled the right information on the basis of which to make his decision. Furthermore, if the group must move on to the next stage or implement the decision, the authority-rule method produces a minimum amount of involvement of the group. Hence it undermines the potential quality of the implementation of the decision.

I have often sat in meetings where the chairman has decided something after listening to the group for a few minutes, but the action taken proved to be somehow out of line with what the chairman wanted. Upon later reconstruction it turned out that the group either misunderstood the decision or did not agree with it in the first place, and hence was neither able nor motivated to carry it out effectively.

3. Decision by Minority One of the most common complaints of group members is that they feel railroaded in reference to some decision. Usually this feeling results from one, two, or three people employing tactics that produce action and therefore must be considered decisions, but which are taken without the consent of the majority.

A single person can railroad a decision, particularly if he is in some kind of chairmanship role, by not giving opposition an opportunity to build up. Let us take an example pertaining to a decision as to how the group should work. The chairman says: "I think the way to go at this is to each state our opinion on the topic to see where we all stand. Now my own opinion is ... " Once he has given his own opinion, he turns to the person on his right and says, "What do you think, Harry?" When Harry has spoken, the chairman points to the next person and the group is off, having made in effect a decision about how it is going to go about its work. Yet no one agreed to this method of work, except the initiator.

Another similar tactic is to say, "Well, we all seem to be agreed, so let's go ahead with John's idea," even though the careful observer may have detected that only John, the chairman, and maybe one other person has spoken favorably about the idea. The others have remained silent. If the initiator is asked how he concluded there was agreement, chances are that he will say, "Silence means consent, doesn't it? Everyone had a chance to voice opposition." If one interviews the group members later, one sometimes discovers that an actual majority was against John's idea but each one hesitated to speak up because he thought that all the other silent ones were for it. They too were trapped by "silence means consent."

Finally, a common form of minority rule is for two or more members to come to quick and powerful agreement on a course of action, to challenge the group with a quick "Does anyone object?", and, if no one raises his voice in two seconds, to proceed with "Let's go ahead, then." Again the trap is the assumption that silence means consent.

The process consultant plays an important role with respect to these first three decision-making methods, primarily because they are rarely labeled as decision-making methods in the first place. Yet a great many group decisions, particularly pertaining to the important issue of group procedures, rules of order, and the like, are made in these rather rapid ways. For a group member to challenge such proceedings, to say, "We don't really agree," is often seen as blocking; hence there are strong pressures on group members to stay silent and let things take their course, even though they are not in agreement.

The consultant must first make the group aware of decisions it has made and the methods by which it has made them;

then he must try to get the group to assess whether they feel that these methods were appropriate to the situation. For example, the members may agree that the chairman did railroad the decision, but they may feel that this was appropriate because time was short and someone needed to make that decision quickly so the group could get on with more important things.

On the other hand, the group might decide that a decision such as having each person in turn state his point of view introduces an element of formality and ritual into the group which undermines its ability to build creatively on ideas already advanced. The group might then wish to choose a different method of idea production. The important thing is to legitimize such process discussion and to have some observations available in case the group is finding it difficult to discern what the consultant is talking about.

4. Decision by Majority Rule: Voting and/or Polling We come next to more familiar decision-making procedures, those which are often taken for granted as applying to any group situation because they reflect our political system. One simple version is to poll everyone's opinion following some period of discussion, and, if a majority feels the same way, to assume that that is the decision. The other method is the more formal one of stating a clear alternative and asking for votes in favor of it, votes against it, and abstentions.

On the surface this method seems completely sound, but surprisingly often decisions made by this method are not well implemented even by the group that made the decision. What is wrong? If one can get the group to discuss its process, or if one interviews members of the minority, it turns out that two kinds of psychological barriers exist: (1) the minority member often feels that there was an insufficient period of discussion for him to really get his point of view across; hence he feels misunderstood and sometimes resentful; (2) the minority member often feels that the voting has created two camps within the group, that these camps are now in win–lose competition, that his camp lost the first round but it is just a matter of time until it can regroup, pick up some support, and win the next time a vote comes up.

In other words, voting creates coalitions, and the preoccupation of the losing coalition is not how to implement what the majority wants but how to win the next battle. If voting is to be used, the group must be sure that it has created a climate in which members feel they have had their day in court and where members feel obligated to go along with the majority decision. A key role for the process consultant is to highlight for the group the pitfalls of each method and to get enough discussion of group climate to ensure that the group will choose an appropriate decision-making process.

5. Decision by Consensus One of the most effective but also most time-consuming methods of group decision making is to seek consensus. Consensus, as I will define it, is not the same thing as unanimity. Rather, it is a state of affairs where communications have been sufficiently open, and the group climate has been sufficiently supportive, to make everyone in the group feel that he has had his fair chance to influence the decision. Someone then tests for the "sense of the meeting," carefully avoiding formal procedures, such as voting.

If there is a clear alternative that most members subscribe to, and if those who oppose it feel they have had their chance to influence the decision, then a consensus exists. Operationally it would be defined by the fact that those members who would not take the majority alternative nevertheless understand it clearly and are prepared to support it. It is a psychological state that might be described as follows:

> I understand what most of you would like to do. I personally would not do that, but I feel that you understand what my alternative would be. I have had sufficient opportunity to sway you to my point of view but clearly have not been able to do so. Therefore, I will gladly go along with what most of you wish to do.

In order to achieve such a condition, time must be allowed by the group for all members to state their opposition and to state it fully enough to get the feeling that others really do understand them. This condition is essential if they are later to free themselves of preoccupation with the idea that they could have gotten their point of view across if others had only understood what they really had in mind. Only by careful listening to the opposition can such feelings be forestalled and effective group decisions reached.

The process consultant can help the group to determine what kinds of decisions should be made by consensus. Which decisions are important enough to warrant the effort? One guideline he might suggest is that procedural decisions, those which pertain to how the group works, are the ones where it is most important that everyone be on board; hence these should probably be made by consensus. The group might decide to give complete authority to the chairman, or it might decide to try for very informal discussion procedures, or it might wish to brainstorm some ideas. But whatever is decided, it should be completely clear to everyone and there should not be residual feelings of being misunderstood or desires to sabotage the group procedure. Unfortunately, this is the kind of decision that most often is made by minorities, costing the group untold hours of wasted effort because of low morale, lack of involvement, and lack of clarity in communication.

6. *Decision by Unanimous Consent* The logically perfect but least attainable kind of decision is where everyone truly agrees on the course of action to be taken. For certain key kinds of decisions it may be necessary to seek unanimity, but for most important ones consensus is enough, if it is real consensus. The process consultant can help the group here by pointing out that the group may be setting too high a standard for itself in some cases. Unanimity is not always necessary and may be a highly inefficient way to make decisions. The important thing is to take some time to agree on which method to use for what kinds of tasks and in what kinds of situations.

A Final Thought

Often the method of decision making is simply announced to the group by the convener or chairman. If this is the case, the process consultant must try to determine whether the group is comfortable with the method being used, and, if not, find an opportunity to raise with the chairman the issue of whether he should permit some discussion by the group of how to handle the decision-making area. In my experience, chairmen often tend to feel threatened by such discussion because they fear that they will lose control of the group and that disorder and chaos will result. One way to reassure them is by pointing out that different ways of making decisions do not necessarily imply a disorderly communication process. If the consultant can provide some viable alternatives, he can often get the chairman to experiment with different methods and draw his own conclusions.

Summary

Problem solving can be thought of as consisting of two cycles, one of which involves primarily discussion and the other primarily action-taking. The first cycle consists of the phases of problem identification and formulation, idea or proposal generation, and idea or proposal testing through attempting to forecast consequences. The most difficult stage is that of identifying and formulating what is really the problem; often this stage requires additional diagnostic effort.

The second cycle involves action planning, action steps, and evaluation of outcomes. The action planning is itself a problem-solving process and should be treated as such. The major difficulty in the total cycle is making the transition from cycle 1 to cycle 2 if different parties are involved. Those who have to implement the decisions should be involved in making them at the earliest possible stage.

The decision process itself can be handled by

1. lack of group response;
2. authority rule;
3. minority rule;
4. majority rule;
5. consensus; and/or
6. unanimity.

It is important for a group to become aware of these different decision-making methods and to learn to choose an appropriate method for the kind of task or decision it is working on.

6

Group Growth
and Development:
Norms and Culture

As a group works together and faces common problems, it gradually builds common assumptions about itself and norms of conduct. In other words, the group as a group learns how to cope with its problems of external survival in its environment and to manage and integrate its internal processes. The sum total of this learning, embodied as a set of implicit assumptions that come to be taken for granted, can be thought of as the "culture" of that group. One of the main aspects of this culture will be the norms that guide group members' behavior.

The process by which norms and, eventually, cultural assumptions develop can be observed if one watches for critical incidents in the group's life and how the group deals with them (Schein, 1985). For example, as a process consultant I often observe that there are moments in the problem-solving process where the manager or someone influential attempts to get his way and one or more other members argue or refuse to go along. Some form of "insubordination" occurs. If the manager reacts punitively and makes it clear that he expects his suggestions to be taken as orders, and if the other group members now cease to argue and accept the punishment, a norm of how to deal with authority has been established.

Or, to give another example, in my observer role I note varying degrees of openness of communication. One group member suddenly says to another, "I think you did a lousy job of handling that customer." How the other group members, especially people in positions of authority, deal with this comment will begin to build a norm around openness and confrontation. If there is a shocked silence and the chairman acts as if nothing had happened and changes the subject, he is sending a clear signal that such openness is not welcome. On the other hand, if he says, "John, I understand how you feel and would like to hear a bit more about what you observed that made you reach this judgment," he is not only accepting such remarks as legitimate, but is furthering the dialogue by asking for additional information. He may also be starting to try to build a norm that judgments are legitimate only if they are backed up by facts and figures.

Norms are not easy to define or to identify in group process, yet they are very influential in determining member behavior, perceptions, and feelings. Part of their influence derives from the fact they operate invisibly, in that they are carried in each member's head as personal guidelines.

A norm can be defined as a set of assumptions or expectations held by the members of a group or organization concerning what kind of behavior is right or wrong, good or bad, appropriate or inappropriate, allowed or not allowed. Norms are usually not articulated spontaneously, but members can state them if asked to do so. For example, some typical norms in a group might be:

"We should not swear or use foul language in this group."

"We should get to meetings on time."

"We should not challenge or question the statements of the chairman of the group."

"We should be informal with each other, use first names."

"Everyone in the group should participate."

"We should reach consensus and not fall back on voting."

"We should not start the meeting until all the members are present."

Those norms which are open, verbalized, or even written down function as the rules and regulations of the group and can for this purpose be called explicit norms. Those which are unspoken can be thought of as implicit norms. We know they are there from observing member reactions when they are violated: shocked silences, rebukes, "Dutch Uncle" talks, and the like. If norms are violated repeatedly, members are punished in various ways and ultimately expelled from the group if their behavior does not conform in critical areas.

One important function of the process consultant is to attempt to decipher norms and to check how much consensus there is in the group on certain issues. In the previous chapter this was identified as the setting and testing of standards. One of the most destructive aspects of group behavior comes about from lack of consensus — when members assume that a norm is operating, but, in fact, none is. Valuable ideas and suggestions are suppressed because members assume that they would not be accepted, leading sometimes to the group doing something that no one really wanted to do. Jerry Harvey (1974) has identified this condition as the Abilene Paradox; he argued persuasively that to avoid going to Abilene when, in fact, no one really wants to go, it is necesary to state and check one's assumptions.

The process consultant can also help the group by observing closely how critical incidents are handled and trying to infer the kinds of norms the group is building for itself. If the group later engages in some process analysis of its own, the consultant can help the group to identify and reconstruct some of its norms and to test for itself whether the norms are helpful or constitute a barrier to effective action. For example, a group may discover that it has built a norm that people should speak up only when asked directly for an opinion or some information. The group may feel that such a formal mode of operating is getting in the way of good idea production. Having identified the norm, the group can then set about to change it explicitly to bring it into line with their feelings about how the group should operate.

The group may also discover that explicit and implicit norms tend to counteract each other. For example, there may be an explicit norm to say exactly what is on one's mind, but an implicit norm that one must not contradict the ideas of certain powerful people in the group. Or there may be an explicit norm that all members of the group are equal and have an equal voice in the discussion, but an implicit norm that higher-status people in the group should speak first and others in the group should try to go along with their views. Such norms can be very subtle in their operation, and the process consultant must be able to identify concrete examples if the group is to learn to observe the effects of the norms for itself.

As norms develop and become interlocked with each other, one can begin to think of the group's "culture." One of the reasons culture is so difficult to change is that when norms begin to support each other, one must change the whole set of norms instead of just the one or two that may be getting in the way. For example, assume that a group has developed the norm that one should always seek consensus on important decisions, and this norm is supported by other norms, such as "One must speak up if one disagrees with the decision that is being made," "One must always be truthful and open in task-oriented discussion," and "One must not try to take an action oneself unless the group has achieved consensus on that action." To change the decision norm toward "One must do what the chairman asks" (perhaps in order to get decisions made more quickly) is not likely to be possible unless people also change their attitudes toward participation and implementation. The process consultant must help the group to see these interconnections so that change processes are undertaken realistically.

Much more could be said about culture, but that would be beyond the scope of this discussion. Suffice it to say that the process consultant must be very mindful of cultural norms because they are so powerful in their operation.[1]

---

[1]The reader wishing more detail and discussion of culture as a topic and its effects on organizational life is referred to *Process Consultation: Volume 2* (1987a) and to my book *Organizational Culture and Leadership* (1985).

Group Growth

Relationships and groups do develop and grow from the early stages of getting acquainted described in Chapter 4 to the mature stages of effective, smooth functioning, and ultimately to stable states and stagnation. But it is often difficult for the members of the group to realize that the group has developed and grown, because the criteria of growth are usually not well defined. The process consultant can be most helpful in identifying for the group some of the ways it has developed and matured.

There is no single criterion that can be universally applied to test the degree of maturity of a group, but there are a number of dimensions along which a group can assess itself in order to identify where it has grown and where it may still need further development. These dimensions can be put into a simple self-rating questionnaire that the members can fill out periodically to determine how they feel about each dimension and how these feelings change over time. A sample of such a questionnaire is shown in Figure 6–1, but there is nothing absolute about the particular dimensions chosen.

The dimensions in Figure 6–1 reflect some of the basic criteria of maturity that have been developed for judging individual personality. Similar criteria can be applied to groups:

1. Does the group have the capacity to deal realistically with its environment, and is it indcpendent of its environment to an optimal degree?
2. Is there basic agreement in the group about mission, goals, and ultimate values?
3. Does the group have a capacity for self-knowledge? Does the group understand why it does what it does?
4. Is there an optimum use of the resources available within the group?
5. Is there an optimum integration of the group's internal processes — communication, decision making, distribution of authority and influence, and norms?
6. Does the group have the capacity to learn from its expe-

A MATURE GROUP POSSESSES:

1. Adequate mechanisms for getting feedback:

   | Poor | 1 | 2 | 3 | 4 | 5 | Excellent feedback |
   feedback   Average   mechanisms
   mechanisms

2. Adequate decision-making procedure:

   | Poor | 1 | 2 | 3 | 4 | 5 | Very adequate deci- |
   decision-   Average   sion making
   making
   procedure

3. Optimal cohesion:

   | Low | 1 | 2 | 3 | 4 | 5 | Optimal cohesion |
   cohesion   Average

4. Flexible organization and procedures:

   | Very | 1 | 2 | 3 | 4 | 5 | Very flexible |
   inflexible   Average

5. Maximum use of member resources:

   | Poor | 1 | 2 | 3 | 4 | 5 | Excellent use of |
   use of   Average   resources
   resources

6. Clear communications:

   | Poor | 1 | 2 | 3 | 4 | 5 | Excellent communi- |
   communi-   Average   cation
   cation

(*continued*)

Figure 6–1
Criteria of Group Maturity

7. Clear goals accepted by members:

Unclear goals— not accepted	1	2	3 Average	4	5	Very clear goals— accepted

8. Feelings of interdependence with authority persons:

No interdependence	1	2	3 Average	4	5	High interdependence

9. Shared participation in leadership functions:

No shared participation	1	2	3 Average	4	5	High shared participation

10. Acceptance of minority views and persons:

No acceptance	1	2	3 Average	4	5	High acceptance

Figure 6–1   *(Continued)*

rience? Can it assimilate new information and respond flexibly to it?

No group is going to achieve some perfect level on all of these dimensions. Their major usefulness is that they permit the group to study its own progress over time and to identify weak spots in how it is operating. This implies capacity to learn and puts special emphasis on criterion number 6 in the above list. One can elaborate this criterion further by identifying what for groups and organizations can be thought of as a healthy learning or coping cycle — the steps that have to be successfully negotiated if the group is to learn from its own experience (Schein, 1980):

1. *Sensing* a change in some part of the environment, either internal or external;
2. *Importing* the relevant information into those parts of the group or organization than can act on it, and *digesting* the information (instead of denying or subverting it);
3. *Changing* internal processes according to the information obtained while, at the same time, reducing or managing the undesirable side effects of the changes made;
4. *Exporting* new behavior or "products" to respond to whatever environmental changes had been sensed;
5. *Obtaining feedback* on the degree to which the new responses successfully deal with the environmental change.

The process consultant can play a crucial role in helping the group to identify these stages of the coping process and to evaluate which steps are well handled and which are poorly handled by the group. It is especially important to identify those areas where the group is doing well and has shown real evidence of growth, because so often members see only the dysfunctional aspects of what they do and get discouraged prematurely about their work with each other.

Summary

The origin, function, and meaning of group norms and culture were discussed. I highlighted the importance that norms have in the life of the group, making norms and norm formation one of the key processes to focus on and track. Some dimensions along which a group can measure its growth and development were identified, and the underlying criteria for group growth and successful group learning were described.

7

Leading and Influencing

All interpersonal relationships involve efforts to lead and influence. We always have intentions and goals, whether they be external task related or simply the need to develop a friendship or have a good time or be liked. How we influence the situation to achieve our goals is, however, one of the most complex and multifaceted processes in the human situation.

This area has been analyzed from the perspective of "leadership," "management," "authority," and "power." It is a confusing area because the premises or assumptions on which influence attempts are usually built remain implicit and often deliberately concealed, leading us to negative influence concepts such as "manipulation" or "coercion."

In order to develop some simplifying models of this complex area, I need first to clarify what I will mean by the key terms:

1. *Leadership:* behavior on the part of some members of the group or organization that creates or changes basic assumptions and values in the group.
2. *Management:* behavior on the part of some members of the group or organization that helps the group to

achieve some goals, but within the assumptions or values previously agreed on by the group.

3. *Power:* the ability to control/influence the behavior of others because of (a) the possession of resources that those others need; (b) personal characteristics (charisma) that make one influential; and/or (c) the perception that one controls resources that others need.

4. *Authority:* the amount of influence that is legitimately granted to an organizational position or to a person; if others do not consent to the basis of legitimacy (promotion, election, and so on), the person may have formal authority but no influence.

5. *Coercion:* the ability to influence others whether or not they consent because of actual control of resources, such as freedom, food, or safety, that those others need.

6. *Manipulation:* influencing others without making visible the motivation behind the influence attempts; the legitimacy of the manipulation is a function of how one would evaluate the motivation.

Given these definitions, how does one now make sense of the multitude of influence attempts one can observe in any human situation? One approach to simplifying this area is to note that historically there have been several major models or sets of assumptions that have guided managerial thought based on our understanding of what went on in organizations. These can be thought of as four "models of human nature" (Schein, 1980).

1. Rational-economic Assumptions This set of assumptions, closely paralleling McGregor's Theory X, is built on the view that human beings work for money, that they must be motivated and controlled by economic incentives, and that, being lazy, without managerial effort they would basically do nothing. Therefore, the manager must motivate, organize, control, and, in effect, bear the responsibility and burden of his subordinates' performance.

2. Social Assumptions This set of assumptions is built on the view that human beings' basic needs are to have good relationships with both fellow workers and supervisors. The manager must therefore set up a congenial work situation, care about his subordinates, understand their needs and go to bat for them, and establish close and harmonious relations with them.

3. *Self-actualizing Assumptions* This set of assumptions is built on the view that human begins have a hierarchy of needs and, as lower-order needs are satisfied, higher-order needs come into play, culminating in the human need to use all of one's potential and thereby to actualize oneself. The manager must therefore provide adequate challenge, a work situation that permits subordinates to use their talents fully, and enough understanding of his subordinates to know when and how to challenge them. There is no need to control and motivate them because the motivation is already there waiting to be released. The capacity for self-control is also already present in humans. This set of assumptions is closely parallel to McGregor's Theory Y.

4. *Complex Assumptions* This set of assumptions is built on the view that human beings are different from each other and that they change and grow in their motives as well as in knowledge and skills. Therefore, a person can start out being rational-economic but learn to be self-actualizing. It will depend on the organization, his personality, and a whole host of other factors. The manager must therefore be a good diagnostician in order to know what the motivations and abilities of his subordinates actually are, and must be flexible enough to use different influence attempts with different people.

The process consultant often has the opportunity to observe a manager in action. He can see him handle people, run groups, issue written memoranda, and think out loud. One way the consultant can attempt to interpret what he hears and observes is to ask himself what underlying assumptions about people the manager holds, and how these assumptions are in turn influencing the manager's leadership style. As opportunities arise to discuss issues, the consultant can then direct the manager's thinking to his own assumptions. The consultant can provide observations and help the manager to interpret the implications of his own behavior.

For example, I have spent some time with a manager who

told me that he wants his immediate subordinates to take more initiative in running their own operations. A little while later he showed me a list of nineteen (!!) questions he had asked of one of these subordinates about a proposal this particular person had made. I asked the manager whether he thought there was any inconsistency between the messages he was sending to his subordinate: "Take more initiative" and, at the same time, "Here are nineteen things you had better think about before you act."

After further exploration, it turned out that the manager really didn't trust his subordinates to the extent he professed. His elaborate questioning attitude was a clear signal of this mistrust. Consequently, subordinates behaved very cautiously. Only after some real exploration of his own behavior did the manager realize that ideally he wanted initiative, but in practice he wanted pretty tight control. Once he recognized these feelings in himself he became less upset over the cautious behavior of his subordinates.

Another example illustrates a more far-reaching organizational phenomenon. A company president who prides himself on creating a climate in which engineers and other professionals really feel challenged by their work was told that the company's internal communications system was being overused and costing too much. He verified the fact of the high costs and then instructed his office manager to issue a memorandum that turned out to be punitive and rather supercilious in its tone. It was as if it had been written for either stupid or recalcitrant people. The president asked me what I thought of it, prior to his sending it out.

The ensuing discussion was aimed at helping this man see the inconsistency between a climate in which people were supposed to be treated as professionals and a memorandum that treated them as if they were recalcitrant children. I argued that if the memorandum went out in its original form, the communications systems might indeed be used less but the climate of professionalism might be irreparably damaged. The president would be sending a message that implied that he didn't really trust his people at all, which would have been quite inconsistent with his actual feelings. Being unused to thinking in terms of the total organizational effects of a managerial communication, he did not initially see the inconsistency. Once he saw it, he could choose the kind of message he was willing to have go out to his organization.

Many managers are, of course, truly ambivalent. They want to trust people and they send signals accordingly; at the same time they are afraid to trust them and unwittingly send out other signals that imply mistrust. The process consultant can help best by encouraging self-examination so that the ambivalence itself comes to be recognized as a real feeling. The manager can then choose whether to lean in one direction or the other, or to continue to be ambivalent. But whatever course he now chooses, he does so with some insight into the probable effects of his behavior on the people around him.

Sources of Power or Bases of Legitimacy

One of the most critical areas to observe is how successful influence attempts actually come about. When A influences B, what is the real reason that B was influenced? Power, influence, and leadership are such complex concepts in part because there is no simple answer to why B was influenced. The reason could be any of several possibilities:

1. *Coercion, nonlegitimate influence:* B went along with what A wanted because he felt he had no choice. A controlled some critical resource B needed, such as his job, or his next raise, or his future in the company.
2. *Tradition:* B went along because he had always gone along with what A wanted because A was by prior history in a position where it was "right" to go along. A might be B's father, or the king in the traditional monarchy, or the founder/owner of the business.
3. *Legitimate authority:* B went along because he accepted A as his legitimate boss. This implies that B accepts the system by which people get to positions of authority, whether that be a system of election or appointment. It is the acceptance of the system that creates legitimacy, so B will take orders even from a boss who may be per-

sonally not respected. But if he is the boss and got there by legitimate means, he is accepted in that role.

4. *Derivative authority:* B went along because A was a friend of someone that B respects or was appointed by B's legitimate boss, or in some other way derives his authority from someone else who granted him power.

5. *Expertise:* B went along because he respects A's ability to solve problems of the sort that are at issue. B has learned from past observation of A that A has the expertise and knowledge, and, therefore, can be trusted to give sensible orders.

6. *Personality or charisma:* B went along because A was such a powerful pesonality that B could not resist. In fact, he may develop a blind loyalty to A and do even things that do not make sense if A has the kind of personality that commands admiration and allegiance.

Which of these various sources of power or influence was involved makes a difference in how B feels, how stable the situation is in the long run, and how well implemented the decision will be. If B feels that the influence attempt was not legitimate, he may agree but sabotage the decision or implement it with so little effort and enthusiasm that it will not solve the problem. The process consultant must therefore help the manager/leader to understand on what basis his power or authority rests. If he miscalculates in this area, he risks becoming ineffective.

It is particularly risky if the manager attributes to himself more legitimacy, expertise, or charisma than he in fact has. If the subordinate goes along because of coercion or tradition, the boss may be fooled into thinking that the relationship is stable and that implementation will be effective when, in fact, neither of these conditions will hold. The consultant must help the manager to think realistically about the source of his influence.

Leadership and Decision-Making Style

We have previously referred to the different means by which groups make decisions. Looking at this process from the

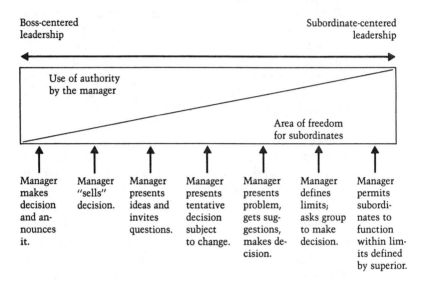

Figure 7-1
A Continuum of Managerial Behavior *

*Tannenbaum, R., and Schmidt, W. H., "How to choose a leadership pattern." *Harv. Bus. Rev.*, March-April, 1958.

perspective of the manager, we can now analyze what options are open to him when he must initially structure an interpersonal situation. This issue applies to staff meetings, task forces, or any kind of situation where some people are brought together for the eventual solution of a problem. The most useful formulation of the action alternatives available to the manager has been provided by Tannenbaum and Schmidt (1958). They identify a basic dimension that runs from *total leader autocracy* on one end to *total group autonomy* on the other end (see Fig. 7-1). At one extreme the manager makes the decision and simply announces it to the others involved; at the other extreme the manager states the ultimate target to be achieved but gives the group complete freedom in how to achieve it.

Most managers recognize these extremes readily. What they are less likely to recognize is that there are a number of in-between positions and that one can choose different positions at different times. For example, the manager can make the decision himself but make a real effort to explain and sell it to others. He can retain the power to make the decision but tell the group what his ideas are and invite comment prior to making the decision. Still further along on the continuum, he can present the problem and invite ideas and alternatives from the group prior to making a decision, or he can let the group know of several alternatives among which they might choose. He can state some limits outside of which the group may not go but permit the group to decide within those limits. And he can vary his behavior from one decision to the next.

What factors will determine the appropriate position for any given managerial situation? Tannenbaum and Schmidt identify three sets of forces that should be considered:

1. Forces in the leader himself
2. Forces in the subordinates
3. Forces in the situation

Examples of forces in the leader are his value system, his confidence in the group, his own natural inclinations or style, and the security he feels in the situation. Examples of forces in the group are their prior experience in making decisions, their actual competence, their tolerance for ambiguity, their ability to become involved in the problem, and their expectations and need for growth. Examples of forces in the situation are the amount of time pressure, the type of problem to be solved, and the type of organization in which the process is occurring.

The process consultant can be most useful in helping the manager to see the alternatives available to him and to make a diagnosis of the various forces that have been outlined. There are no right or wrong assumptions about people in the abstract, and there is no right or wrong leadership style in the abstract. The problem for the manager is to make an accurate diagnosis and choose a course of action appropriate to that diagnosis.

It should be noted that this kind of leadership/managerial

model says relatively little about the traits or characteristics of the leader. I do not believe that there is some magic set of traits that can be identified in all leaders, nor do I believe that all leadership/managerial situations call for the same mix of traits. The unique requirements for being a good president may be quite different from the requirements for a good vice president. The production manager often has to be a different type of person from a sales manager or a research manager. (Each may wish to be a leader, but what he must do to lead effectively varies with the job and the situation.)

Given the above ideas, the process consultant cannot really help a company to identify who should be in what job or who should be promoted. Indeed, his initial psychological contract with the organization would probably preclude involvement in such activities. On the other hand, the consultant might be most useful by helping a manager to think through whether his own traits, values, motives, and temperament are suited for a particular kind of leadership position he is in or aspires to be in. If he has observed the manager in action, he can certainly provide observations that may help the manager to think more clearly about his own style and select a leadership pattern that fits him best. If he finds incompatibilities between job demands and his personal style, he can then, on his own, seek a niche where his style matches job requirements better.

Leading versus Managing

In the above discussion I have used leadership, management, and influence more or less interchangeably. If one wants to distinguish these concepts I would propose that leading and managing both involve influence, but that leadership implies influencing ultimate goals, mission, and culture, while management implies influencing how things are implemented and carried out. As Warren Bennis has put it very succinctly: Managers do things right; leaders to the right thing (Bennis and Nanus, 1985).

I have also argued that leadership involves the unique function of assesing and, if necessary, changing organizational culture. If the process consultant finds himself in a situation where leaders need help in this process, he can be most helpful by providing diagnostic tools to help assess what the culture is and help in the implementation of change processes. Most likely such help will involve getting the leader to see how difficult and traumatic culture change can be for the members of an organization (Schein, 1985).

Summary

Leading, managing, and influencing have been identified as highly variable kinds of behavior resting on many different kinds of implicit assumptions. Effective behavior depends on the person, his subordinates, the nature of the task to be accomplished, and the organizational setting within which the process takes place. Therefore, no easy generalizations can be made about influence processes, except that they are highly contingent on the particulars of the situation.

The kinds of assumptions that the leader/manager holds about people will determine to a large extent how he will attempt to influence them. Becoming aware of one's own assumptions is therefore crucial, and helping others to become aware of their assumptions is essential. The leader/manager has a choice within his assumption set of how tightly to centralize control and how flexible to be from one decision to the next. By diagnosing the forces in himself, his subordinates, and the situation, he can increase his flexibility and, thereby, his effectiveness.

8

Appraising Performance and Giving Feedback

The process consultant will observe in any human organization a constant stream of judgments that people make about each other. Sometimes these judgments will be articulated publicly, that is, will be "fed back" to the person about whom they are made. Often they are made privately. One of the most common dilemmas for the process consultant is what to say when after a meeting the manager asks him what he "thinks of so-and-so."

In order for the consultant to think clearly about this, he must have a model of how human behavior and performance can be measured and evaluated, and what the pitfalls are in this process.

Why Are People and Their Performance Appraised?

It is intrinsic to organizational life and to the process of management that evaluations are made of individual employees. But why? Who needs this information and why do we gather it?

Most managers would give one or more of the following reasons for appraising performance:

1. *As a basis for personnel actions.* Every organization needs to know whom to select for a given job, whom to promote, how to distribute limited rewards among several people doing similar jobs, whom to transfer out, and whom to terminate.
2. *As a basis for human resource planning.* Every organization needs some kind of process for ensuring that it will have the right number of people with the right mix of talents at some point in the future.
3. *As a basis for individual development planning.* Most organizations want to maximize their pool of human talent, so they need some system for identifying who needs what kind of development. Such information is also necessary to facilitate whatever career counseling is needed in connection with development.
4. *To improve performance.* The most fundamental reason for performance appraisal, of course, is to ensure that everyone's performance will improve so that the overall effectiveness of the total organization will improve.

Awareness of these multiple purposes should alert the process consultant to the fact that different kinds of information and appraisal processes may be relevant to these different purposes. No one system may meet all of the needs. So when a manager is seeking help in appraising someone, the consultant might well start with the question "For what purpose or purposes are you trying to make a judgment here?"

What Is Appraisal?

The next question to be addressed is "What do we mean by appraisal, anyway?" This process can be broken down into four logically distinguishable steps:

1. Some *observations* of the behavior of the person being judged, hopefully in situations that are performance related.

2. The *evolution of some standard or criterion* that defines very high levels, expected levels, and substandard levels of performance.
3. Some *comparison* of the observed behavior with the standard or the criterion, implying some ability to measure or rate the behavior and the criterion.
4. Some *judgment* or *assessment* of what the gap between the observed behavior and the criterion means evaluatively.

The process consultant should be aware that in practice these steps tend to be collapsed into instant judgments, such as "Joe is one of my best men," "Pete is messing up," or "Jane can't handle people." Instead of being seduced into agreeing or disagreeing, the consultant should help the manager to surface each of the above questions — what data is he basing his judgment on, what standard is he using and why, how does the person in fact compare to the standard, and so what? If the consultant can help the manager to think through each of the steps and check out the client's logic, he is helping him to make evaluations without having to make evaluations himself on minimal data.

What Is Appraised?

To complicate matters further, it is often not clear just what the manager is, in fact, looking at when he makes an appraisal. Several categories of information can be identified:

1. *Stable traits.* These are usually personality or skill characteristics that are presumed to be unchangeable, for example, "He is a very dynamic person," "He lacks aggressiveness," "She is one of our best computer people."
2. *Malleable traits.* These are personality or skill characteristics that are presumed to be changeable through experience or training, for example, "He comes on too strong with people, but may well mellow with experience," "She needs to become more assertive in meetings," "Right now all she lacks is self-confidence."
3. *Averaged performance.* This is a summary over a period

of time of some specific behavioral characteristic or result, for example, "He always does a good job with our customers," "She handles the pressure of the job very well," "She has done consistently high-quality work with our key accounts."

4. *Specific performance.* This is an appraisal of a specific situation, for example, "She handled the shop steward very well at that meeting," "His presentation to the group was weak and lacking in conviction," "She missed the deadline for the sales promotion."

5. *Future potential.* This is an assessment of strengths and weaknesses relative to future jobs. At one extreme, potential is simply an assessment of whether the person is promotable to the next higher level or to a different function (promotability). At the other extreme, potential refers to how many promotions the person might be able to handle and to what goal job he could aspire (ultimate potential).

The consultant should be alert to possible confusion that can arise when the evaluator is not clear about what kind of information he is using for what purpose. For example, if the goal is to improve performance, the most relevant information is specific performance feedback (category 4 above). If the goal is human resource planning, averaged performance and potential become more relevant. If salary action or promotion is the issue, malleable traits and averaged performance are the most relevant. And if personal development is the issue, a discussion of stable and malleable traits is most relevant. The consultant does not have to get into the evaluator role in order to be helpful to the manager in thinking through the evaluation process with the aid of categories such as those shown above.

Giving and Receiving Performance Feedback

One of the major issues surrounding the appraisal process is what happens to the evaluative information. Is it simply entered into personnel records and kept under lock and key, or is it revealed to the person? And if it is revealed, how much is revealed?

The norms in the organization around the issue of openness of appraisal information can become complicated because the feedback norms and the manner in which appraisal is done interact with each other. To be specific, if the organization has clear norms that "one should fully disclose to the employee everything that is said about that employee in the appraisal process," it is predictable that the appraisal process itself will gravitate toward less extreme judgments and evaluations. Supervisors will not make extreme judgments in the first place if they know that they will feel uncomfortable discussing them with the subordinate.

If, on the other hand, the organization has clear norms that one need not give employees anything more than very generalized feedback and can withhold whatever the organization considers to be privileged information, one will get a much more honest, true assessment, but employees will not benefit from it except as they do or do not get raises, promotions, and transfers.

The situation now becomes paradoxical as the different goals of the appraisal process as outlined earlier lead to conflicting procedures. If one wants the most accurate information for personnel actions and human resource planning, the system should be biased toward minimizing feedback to employees; but if one wants to improve performance and employee development, the system should be biased toward maximizing feedback to employees. No one set of procedures will fulfill both sets of goals effectively.

How can the process consultant help managers get out of this box? The most important point to recognize is that the conflict is intrinsic because of the inherent difficulty of giving feedback about performance. The consultant can be supportive to managers by helping them to recognize that reluctance to appraise and give feedback is a normal response in most cultures because of the wider social norms about protecting "face."

The manager must then be helped to figure out which of the goals of performance appraisal are, in fact, the most important, and then how to achieve those. Since performance improvement is likely to be high on the list, and since that always involves learning to give some kind of feedback to the employee, the manager can be helped to develop his skills in giving performance feedback.

The consultant can also raise the question of whether or not a single appraisal system can fulfill all of the needed functions, and, if necessary, help managers to develop several systems. In many organizations there is a performance appraisal system that maximizes feedback and a separate human resource planning system that emphasizes promotability and potential, the data from which are not shared with employees except in general form.

In any case, the skills of giving feedback are central to the appraisal process and, since they are also critical to the activities of the process consultant, he is in a good position to do some coaching on how best to give feedback. I have found it useful in this context to give a short lecture on giving and receiving feedback that emphasizes the following points.

Giving Feedback: Problems, Pitfalls, and Guidelines

Feedback can be defined as information that provides the recipient guidance concerning whether or not he is on target relative to some goal that he is trying to achieve. Feedback always implies some goals on the part of the recipient. Therefore, the first and most important pitfall is

1. *Failure to agree on goals to be achieved and/or performance standards to be met.*

If the boss and the subordinate disagree on goals and performance standards, what may be corrective information from the point of view of the boss may be irrelevant criticism from the point of view of the subordinate.

Feedback can emphasize positives (things the subordinate did well), be descriptive and neutral (things the subordinate did, without any judgment or evaluation), or emphasize negatives (things the subordinate did not do well). Most learning theory has shown that the consequences of the three types of information are different.

Positive feedback is easiest to learn from and most pleasant in that it guides future behavior directly into more of what is already effective. *Descriptive neutral feedback* can be effective if the subordinate has clear standards and only needs to know what he did. In areas where people are very sensitive and "ego-involved," this may be the only kind of information they can accept.

Negative feedback is often necessary in order to ensure that certain kinds of behavior will not be repeated, but it is also the most problematic because of the likelihood that it will arouse defensiveness, be denied or not heard, and in other ways rejected. Furthermore, negative feedback does not offer any guidance on what the person should do and hence does not provide a learning direction.

The second pitfall in the feedback process, then, is

2. *Overreliance on negative feedback and insufficient descriptive and positive feedback.*

Feedback is a communication process subject to all of the pitfalls of communication as outlined in Chapter 3. Basic lack of clarity in the feedback message or semantic confusion when personality traits are involved are therefore potential problems, as illustrated below.

The third pitfall in the feedback process, then, is

3. *Vagueness and generality in the message instead of specific examples and guidelines.*

Several examples will make clear what I mean by these two points. In each of the examples I am deliberately highlighting the pitfalls.

Unclear: "You are too aggressive" (negative, vague, general).

Clear: "I have observed you shouting other people down when they are trying to express their own views, and I think this may undermine communication" (descriptive, precise, specific).

Unclear: "You don't handle your people well" (negative, general).

Clear: "You should involve your subordinates more in making decisions and give them a chance to express their own views" (negative, specific).

Unclear: "You need to show more initiative" (negative, general).

Clear: "Instead of waiting for me to discover that your costs are overrunning, you should set up your own systems for finding this out and correct it before it goes too far" (positive, specific).

The key to semantic clarity is specificity. The more general the comment, whether positive or negative, the more likely it is to be misunderstood.

The next problem with feedback has to do with the perceived motivation of the giver of feedback. If the recipient believes that the giver is genuinely interested in helping the recipient, he is more likely to listen and pay attention than if he has doubts about or mistrusts those motives. We have all had the experience of feeling angry with someone and, as a way of expressing the anger, saying, "Let me give you some feedback." Needless to say, the receiver senses that the giver's needs are being served more than the receiver's. The fourth pitfall in giving feedback, then, is

4. *Lack of clarity about the giver's motives.*

Again, several examples will make clear what is involved.

Confused: "You should motivate your subordinates to control their costs more because this quarter we have again gone beyond our budget" (the boss wants to improve performance, but the subordinate feels he has been criticized for continuing to be a poor manager and gets preoccupied with career issues).

Clear: "Basically the operation is going well, but I continue to worry about the fact that we are again overrunning our budget; what suggestions do you have for getting your subordinates to be more cost-conscious?" (the boss makes his own feelings clear and focuses on the specific issue with a specific question).

Confused: "I think you need to learn to handle customers

better" (the boss may perceive the subordinate to be a person of high potential who has to overcome only one area of weakness, but the subordinate may perceive himself to be generally failing and, therefore, become defensive).

Clear: "You are already very effective and could improve that effectiveness even more if you concentrated on learning how to handle customers better" (the boss makes clear his motive to make already good performance even better).

Confused: "I could get you only a 5 percent raise this year because things are generally lean in the company" (the boss is trying to be truthful, but the subordinate may conclude that he is being subtly told that he is only an average performer and become demoralized).

Clear: "Your performance overall was excellent this last year, and I wish I could reward it with money, but the company has had a generally lean year, so no one got more than a 5 percent raise" (the boss is being specific and puts the subordinate performance into the proper context).

A closely related problem in giving feedback is the natural tendency not to want to be critical because criticism so often produces defensiveness and unpleasant hassle. Or, even more serious, critical comments are denied or not heard at all, thus making all of the effort to give negative feedback seemingly a waste of time. The fifth pitfall, then, is

5. *Withholding of negative critical information in order to avoid hassle.*

What the consultant must learn and what he can teach to the manager is that the solution here, as in the above cases, is to substitute clear, specific examples for vague generalities. I can accept criticism of some specific behavior in a specific situation, but find it much harder to accept criticism of my traits and more general characteristics. In the former case I can attribute my behavior to situational circumstances and learn how to avoid such behavior; in the latter case my self-image and self-esteem become involved and I cannot readily change general parts of my personality. Hence I will resist or deny the criticism.

On the other hand, if the negative feedback deals with some concrete behavior that both the giver and receiver have witnessed, the giver can express his own feelings about the behavior and his evaluation of it, and the receiver can avoid ego-involvement. In other words, if I am angry at *you*, this may be a problem for you, but if I am angry at something specific that *you did*, you may get some new insights from that feedback. Some examples of how to give negative criticisms follow.

General trait oriented: "We need more team players at higher levels in this company, and your performance so far has made me doubt whether you want to be or can be enough of a team player."

Specific behavior oriented: "My problem in seeing you move ahead into higher levels of this company is that whenever you get into a group, you immediately want to take over, like in the XYZ committee. And when you were on the ABC task force, the group never made its best possible contribution because your loyalty to your department made the discussions into win–lose debates. When I see you putting down others that way, it makes me angry and I worry about whether or not you can learn enough new behaviors to move ahead in the company."

General trait oriented: "You really lack initiative; you are just not aggressive enough for this kind of work."

Specific trait oriented: "Several things have concerned me about your performance this past year. When we got stuck on the ABC project, you seemed willing to let matters drift instead of coming up with some proposals for how to move forward and confront the problems. When the other division challenged the direction you were going, you backed off instead of showing them why your solution was the right one. I have seen both of these patterns on other projects and am concerned about the lack of initiative and aggressiveness that is implied by such behavior."

In the above examples, the giver did make evaluative comments, but they were directed at specific behavior instead of at the total person. When goals and standards are clear and have been agreed to, such evaluations are sound. But if such agreement does not exist, feedback will work better if it stays descriptive. The giver and receiver can then jointly evaluate the behavior.

In either case, specificity is the key. The more general the evaluation, the more likely it is to be misunderstood, resisted, denied, and the trigger to defensive behavior.

The next pitfall, then, is

6. *Evaluations are applied to general traits or the total person, instead of specific situations and behaviors.*

Many of the examples given above make this point in arguing for specificity. What can be especially devastating is when a general target becomes the object of feelings and judgment as well.

Unsafe: "You really blew it at the last sales meeting; we almost had it sewed up until you stuck your oar in and made the client back off."

Safer: "When you brought up that XYZ issue at the last sales meeting, I thought you really blew it; we almost had it sewed up until your comments were made, and they seemed to make the client back off" (the emphasis is shifted to the person's behavior, and the giver softens his evaluation by making it his own opinion rather than an absolute judgment).

If the subordinate is to learn from the feedback, the message must somehow be related by the receiver to himself. If the feedback comes too long after the event, the receiver may not remember the incident and thus be able to deny it. Or if the feedback is too general, the receiver may not know to what it refers. Specificity has already been dealt with, but timeliness has not. The next pitfall, then, is

7. *The feedback is poorly timed.*

Proper timing has two components. As previously mentioned, feedback should come soon enough after a given event so that both receiver and giver can clearly remember what happened. Perhaps even more important, however, is that the receiver be ready to listen to feedback. If the *giver* decides when to give it, he may encounter a preoccupied, nervous, or defensive receiver. On the other hand, if the *receiver* decides when to receive feedback, he will make himself psychologically ready to listen. The giver who is concerned about this issue will, therefore, attempt to create a situation where the receiver can take the initiative on when to hold the feedback session. The boss can say that he wants to discuss performance sometime in the next few days and allow the subordinate to pick the time.

The final point about feedback is that it should deal primarily with malleable behavior so that the receiver can do something about what he has been told. On the other hand, if some stable characteristic of the person prevents him from attaining some goals that he desires, it may, on occasion, be necessary for someone to tell him this rather than allowing him to live with illusions and unrealistic expectations.

Process Consultation as Feedback Management

In concluding this chapter it can be noted that much of what the process consultant does when he intervenes with individuals or groups is manage the feedback process. He makes observations that provide feedback information, he asks questions that direct the client's perception to the consequences of his own behavior, he makes suggestions that have implicit evaluations built into them (any given suggestion implies that other things that have not been suggested are less appropriate than what has been suggested).

The process consultant must therefore be highly aware of the psychological dynamics of appraising human behavior and providing feedback about it. In fact his skill in this area is one of the most important things to pass on to his clients so that they can improve the management of their own organizations.

9

Intergroup Processes

One of the most important and least studied aspects of organizational process is intergroup relations within an organization. Whether or not groups form in organizations is no longer an issue. The evidence is overwhelming that they do — along formal departmental lines, along geographical lines, and in terms of who has to interact with whom in the course of getting the work done. It is also well known that groups develop norms, members feel loyal to their groups and adopt the norms, and the goals of different groups sometimes run at cross-purposes with each other.

Not only do groups develop cultures over a period of time, but the larger cultures of the society, the occupation, the community, and the organization all influence the formation of those cultures and define to some degree how groups should relate to each other. In a capitalist society in which free market competition is the norm for economic enterprises, it is not surprising that groups within organizations similarly tend to be competitive with each other.

Nor is it surprising that most managerial theories encourage such competition on the grounds that it increases motivation and, thereby, productivity. I have often found myself being asked to advise managers on how they could introduce more of a competitive element into their organization by having departments and groups be measured against the same standard and rewarding the winners. This has long been an individual motivational tool, especially in sales departments; that the same tool would seem to be attractive in the intergroup context is not surprising.

What is relatively less well known is that the long- and short-run consequences of intergroup competition may be *dysfunctional* to organizational performance. For one thing, not all managers agree that competition, even though it increases motivation, is good for improving the quality of solutions. In the rush to win, perhaps groups compromise on quality. Or some kinds of groups, such as sales departments in independent regions, can constructively compete, but if the groups are the manufacturing department and the sales department, having them compete would produce obvious problems since they are so interdependent.

Studying Intergroup Processes

Part of the problem of making sense of this area is that the key processes are relatively invisible. If the engineering department has poor relations with the production department, the production workers might be motivated *not* to correct errors that they find in the drawings given to them. Douglas McGregor told of standing at the end of a production line with the foreman watching finished trucks roll off the line. The foreman was comfortably puffing his pipe as he said with faint amusement in his voice, "Well, there she goes . . . but she'll be back."

The ultimately bad product is visible enough, but the lack of interest on the part of the production worker (who failed to correct what he knew was a fault) is hard to observe; it is a private decision on his part *not* to do something. Similarly, the giving of false information or the withholding of information, which typically results from groups competing with each other in a win–lose situation, is difficult to observe, even when one suspects strongly that it exists.

The process consultant can use a variety of techniques in an effort to learn about and intervene in such intergroup processes:

1. He can interview members of each group about their feelings toward the other group and inquire how they translate these feelings into overt behavior.

2. He can try to observe meetings or settings where members of both groups are present and assess the degree of openness of communication, spirit of cooperation, and so on.

3. He can try to theorize what should happen between the groups and check his theories by observing specific situations. For example, if relationships are good, he would theorize that errors by one group would be sympathetically and helpfully dealt with by the other group. He can then try to find an incident where an error occurred and either observe what happens, or, if the incident is past, ask what happened at the time.

4. A final and more complicated method for assessing and working on intergroup processes is to arrange an intergroup exercise of some sort. One model that was developed by Robert Blake and Jane Mouton (1961) involves the following steps:

   a. Each group separately describes its own image of itself and its image of the other group.

   b. Through representatives these images are then reported by each group to the other. Both groups now have some new data about how they are perceived by each other. During the reports each group must just listen, no matter how upset they might be about what they are hearing.

   c. The next stage is not to react, but to meet separately to consider what kind of behavior on the part of each group may have led to the image the other group holds. This forces each group to take the stance of the other group and consider sympathetically how the group might have arrived at its conclusions.

   d. These behavioral hypotheses are then shared and discussed openly by both groups. Only at this step is interaction between the groups allowed.

e. In the final stage the groups work together toward reducing the discrepancy between self-image and the image held by the other group, by planning how to relate differently to each other in future contacts.

This process brings both groups into the common task of exploring why discrepancies of perceptions exist, and thus reduces the competitive task each group faces in trying to outdo the other group and show up well with the rest of the organization or higher-level authorities.

It is particularly important for the higher-level manager to understand intergroup processes because he often has the choice of whether to reward competition, collaboration, or complete independence. Since the most common tendency appears to be to arrange competitive conditions, the process consultant must often attempt to get across some of the possible consequences of competition *before the win–lose situation arises.* These consequences have been derived from laboratory and field experiments and can be reliably reproduced in simulations that involve two groups in win–lose competition.

What happens as a result of competition can be studied in the simulation before a decision is reached, during open competition, and after one group has won out over the other. The kinds of results described below seem to occur no matter what kind of task is given to the groups.

What Happens Within Each Competing Group in the Early Phase?

1. Each group becomes more closely knit and elicits greater loyalty from its members; members close ranks and bury some of their internal differences.
2. The group climate changes from informal, casual, playful, to work and task oriented; concern for members'

psychological needs declines while concern for task accomplishment increases.

3. Leadership patterns tend to change from more democratic toward more autocratic; the group becomes more willing to tolerate autocratic leadership.
4. Each group becomes more highly structured and organized.
5. Each group demands more loyalty and conformity from its members in order to be able to present a solid front.

What Happens Between the Competing Groups?

1. Each group begins to see the other groups as the enemy rather than merely a neutral object.
2. Each group begins to experience distortions of perception: it tends to perceive only the best parts of itself, denying its weaknesses, and tends to perceive only the worst parts of the other group, denying its strengths. Each group is likely to develop a negative stereotype of the other ("they don't play fair the way we do").
3. Hostility toward the other group increases, while interaction and communication with the other group decreases; thus it becomes easier to maintain negative stereotypes and more difficult to correct perceptual distortions.
4. If the groups are forced into interaction — for example, if they are forced to listen to representatives plead their own and the others' cause in reference to some task — each group is likely to listen more closely to their own representative and not to listen to the representative of the other group, except to find fault with his presentation. In other words, group members tend to listen only for that which supports their own position and stereotype.

After a decision has been rendered what happens to the winner and loser?

What Happens to the Winner?

1. The winner retains its cohesions and may become even more cohesive.
2. The winner tends to release tension, lose its fighting spirit, become complacent, casual, and playful (the condition of being "fat and happy").
3. The winner tends toward high intragroup cooperation and concern for members' needs, and low concern for work and task accomplishment.
4. The winner tends to be complacent and to feel that winning has confirmed the positive stereotype of itself and the negative stereotype of the "enemy" group. There is little incentive or basis for reevaluating perceptions, or reexamining group operations in order to learn how to improve them, hence the winner does not learn very much about itself.

What Happens to the Loser?

1. If the outcome is not entirely clear-cut and permits a degree of interpretation (if, for example, the decision was rendered by judges who may be seen as biased, or if the outcome was very close), there is a strong tendency for the loser to *deny* or *distort the reality of losing.* Instead, the loser will find psychological escapes, such as "the judges were biased," "the judges didn't really understand our solution," "the rules of the game were not clearly explained to us," "if luck had not been against us at the one key point, we would have won," and so on. In effect, the loser's first response is to say, "We didn't really lose."
2. If the loss is psychologically accepted, the losing group tends to seek someone or something to blame. Strong forces toward scapegoating are set up. If no outsider can be blamed, the group turns on itself, splinters, surfaces previously unresolved conflicts, fights within itself, all in the effort to find a cause for the loss.
3. The loser is more tense, ready to work harder, and des-

perate to find a new positive direction (the condition of being "lean and hungry").
4. The loser tends toward low intragroup cooperation, low concern for members' needs, and high concern for recouping by working harder in order to win the next round of the competition.
5. The loser tends to learn a lot about itself as a group because its positive stereotype of itself and its negative stereotype of the other group are disconfirmed by the loss, forcing a reevaluation of perceptions; as a consequence, the loser is likely to reorganize and become more cohesive and effective, once the loss has been accepted realistically.

It is far easier to prevent reactions and feelings such as these by not arranging a competitive reward structure in the first place than to undo them once they have become established. The process consultant must find ways of bringing relevant data to the attention of the manager so he can see for himself that a motivational system that seems sound can have pitfalls.

For example, in the Apex Company there was a time when the group was considering how to organize. I was prompted to write a short memo outlining some of the costs and benefits of competition (see Appendix C) as a way of focusing the discussion on this issue. The main effect of this memo was to strengthen the position of those managers who already had misgivings about competitive relationship but needed support for that position since it is so easy to argue for competition.

If the situation is already competitive because of prior management decisions and now is becoming dysfunctional or destructive, remedial measures such as those mentioned at the beginning of this chapter may have to be tried. In the Apex Company such a condition arose when the product lines found themselves in competition with each other and with the sales department, because the product line was rewarded for how much of *its product* was sold, while sales was rewarded for *total sales.*

Consequently, sales effort was assigned not according to product line marketing plans and budgets but according to what the sales department could most easily sell. Certain products were getting too little attention, causing product line managers to become bitter at sales, while sales considered the product lines to be too autocratic and irrational.

After several years of infighting leading to a serious deterioration of relationships between the regional sales managers and the product line managers, the head of personnel (who was OD oriented) proposed to run an intergroup exercise of the type outlined above. My help was sought as the outsider who could stage-manage the process and provide the necessary theory to help groups to understand the dynamics better. The two groups met in a nearby hotel for a day and a half.

The first half day was devoted to preparing self-images and images of the other group, and sharing of these. In the afternoon the groups worked on hypotheses of why they were perceived the way they were, and in the evening they shared these and discussed far into the night how things could have gotten so out of hand. Later the groups described this night session as "getting all the garbage out of the system." It was a highly emotional evening that revealed many false assumptions and stereotypes that had grown up over the years. Just the sharing made both groups aware that they had not been serving the company's or their own interests very well by the manner in which they were dealing with each other.

The next half day was spent organizing how both sales and product lines could maximize their efforts in the future by trying to be more collaborative in a structure that made competition easier but destructive. Several new structures were invented, such as specialty salesmen for those products that required extra focusing in the marketplace, and budget reviews that allowed product lines to negotiate more effectively when they felt their products were being ignored. If sales could get information quickly to the product lines on why customers were not interested, the product lines could alter their marketing effort.

The groups agreed that they needed quarterly meetings to review the new collaborative procedures, clear new garbage out of the system, reestablish communication and trust, and redesign the structure further as needed. The new systems worked, although the quarterly meetings were indeed necessary to keep trust and communication at a high level. It proved to be far harder to undo the damage of prior competition than either group had believed possible.

Other Organizational Processes

The process consultant finds himself, through his observation of managerial behavior, witness to a variety of other organizational processes besides the ones we have reviewed. For example, he sees how managerial decisions in the areas of accounting, budgeting, and controlling will signal to the organization the degree to which subordinates are or are not trusted. The manner in which managers administer performance-appraisal plans or bonus plans also communicates a great deal about their assumptions, and therefore has an immediate as well as long-range effect on the organization. The kind of career planning that is done, the use of training or development activities, and the policies for recruitment and job placement all have implications for how people will feel, relate to each other, and carry out their work.

It is beyond the scope of this volume to treat each of these process areas in detail. For the present I merely wish to note that there are a variety of other processes to which the consultant must pay attention and which he must assess if he is to help the organization become more effective. I have deliberately concentrated on the more immediate kinds of processes that one sees in face-to-face relationships because these are the most accessible and the most likely to produce important behavior change. If organization members can change their behavior in their immediate relations, this will inevitably produce more far-reaching effects organizationally. Even more important, if managers can learn how to diagnose organizational processes better, they can continue to modify their behavior after the consultant is no longer present.

Summary

We have looked briefly at some intergroup and total organizational processes. Of special importance are the conditions that are set up for groups within organizations leading to competition or collaboration. The problems of internal competition were spelled out, and I noted how much more difficult it is to undo these effects than to avoid them in the first place. The process consultant must play an active role in encouraging managers to think through their approach to intergroup relations.

Part III
The Consulting Process in Action

We have now reviewed the major process issues that the consultant should be familiar with, and can shift the focus to the consultation activity as such. What is involved in a typical consulting project, and how should the process consultant think about its various stages and issues? The word *project* should be viewed here only in the most general sense in that PC is a very open ended activity that is usually not formalized in terms of contracts, timetables, or project definitions. Nevertheless, there are steps and stages that characterize the PC relationship that can be described and analyzed:

1. Initial contact with the client organization
2. Defining the relationship, psychological contract
3. Selecting a setting and method of work
4. Diagnostic interventions and data gathering
5. Confrontive interventions
6. Reducing involvement and termination

These stages are not easily defined in terms of periods of time. Rather, they are logically distinct areas with which the consultant must be concerned. Many of the stages, such as 2, 3, 4, and 5, go on simultaneously and involve perpetual renegotiation of the psychological contract. For purposes of exposition, however, they will be presented in the next few chapters in a linear fashion.

10

Establishing Contact
and Defining a Relationship

Initial Contact with the Client

Initial contact is made when someone from the client organization (contact client) telephones or writes me about some problem that he is experiencing or perceives in some part of his organization. Usually he comes to me for one of a number of reasons:

1. He has heard me give a talk on a topic that is related to his perceived problem.
2. He has read a paper or a book of mine.
3. He has become acquainted with me during a training program in which I was an instructor.
4. He has been referred to me by one of my colleagues.
5. He has been referred to me by another client or by someone else in his organization who is acquainted with me.

The contact client indicates that he perceives a problem that he feels is not being solved by normal organizational procedures, or he sees a lack that cannot be filled by present organizational resources.

For example, in Case A, the Apex Manufacturing Company, the contact client was a division manager one level below the president. The company is a large manufacturing concern, organized into several divisions. The contact client indicated that there were communication problems in the top management group resulting from a recent reorganization. Because the company expected to grow rapidly in the next decade, they felt they should work on these kinds of problems in preparation for their growth.

In Case B, the Boyd Consumer Goods Company, the contact client was a member of the personnel department who had known of my interests for some time, had had other contacts with professors at the Sloan School, and was interested in finding a consultant to help the newly appointed president manage the transition from traditional to more modern techniques of management in his organization.

In Case C, the Central Chemical Company, a large multidivision chemical manufacturing concern, the contact client was a fellow faculty member at MIT who had been working with the company and had learned that its management wished some additional consultation help in instituting a variety of change programs in several of their divisions. This company had originally become interested through reading the works of and hearing Douglas McGregor. They had already built a strong internal personnel staff in one of the divisions and had launched a number of very creative internal change programs. The management felt that continual contact with outside resources would help the total effort.

In Case D, the Delta Manufacturing Company, a large supplier of consumer appliances, the contact client was a member of the company's central personnel staff. He had been working in one of the divisions helping various production groups to develop strong interpersonal collaboration and team spirit. When the division director became interested in a similar activity for himself and his staff, he asked the inside man to find him a consultant who could work with the group.

In most such cases I do not know from the initial contact what the real problem is, and, therefore, only agree to discuss it further at an exploratory meeting. If I have some consultation time available, I schedule such a meeting in the near future. If I do not have time, I either ask if the problem can wait or suggest someone else who might be able to help. Occasionally I agree to an exploratory meeting with the understanding that if anything comes of it, the work will be done at a later time or by someone else.

One of the most important criteria for predicting the likelihood that a useful consultation relationship will result is the initial relationship formed between me and the contact client. I find that I evaluate the degree of openness, spirit of inquiry, and authenticity of communication of the contact client. For example, to evaluate openness, I try to assess the responses I get to some of my initial questions. If I suggest an exploratory meeting, I look for a response that indicates a genuine willingness to sit down and engage in some joint diagnosis.

If the caller seems too certain that he already knows what is wrong, or if he has me miscast as an expert in something that I am not expert in, or if he clearly has a misconception of what a consultant coming from an organizational psychology frame of reference could offer, I am cautious even in suggesting a further meeting, lest we end up wasting time. If the caller seems to want merely reassurance for some course of action he has already embarked on or wants a quick solution to a surface problem, I am reluctant to proceed.

If none of the barriers described above arises, the explora tory meeting becomes the first major step toward the establishing of a relationship. It should be noted, however, that even the suggestion of such a meeting, and the kinds of questions the consultant asks in deciding whether or not to have such a meeting, are already diagnostic interventions that will influence how the contact client perceives and thinks about his problem. The guidelines I use in deciding on questions, therefore, are the assumptions I make about what will be helpful in the here and now situation. My behavior must illustrate at all times my commit ment to establishing a helpful relationship.

This philosophy also implies that the process consultant is indifferent in the immediate situation to whether or not he ends up with a client in the longer term. If in the initial meeting sufficient help is provided so that no further meetings are needed, that is effective consultation. The commercial consultant is at a disadvantage in this regard because he is trying to sell his services for longer-range projects. A process consultant must be free of the pressure to sell so that he can genuinely evaluate whether or not he can be helpful to the client. He must be free to turn down clients who would not benefit from this kind of help.

As can be seen, PC cannot start until someone in the organization accepts the assumption that relationships and interpersonal processes that accompany organizational problem solving are important targets for learning. Gaining entry to an organization in the role of process consultant is, therefore, highly contingent on one or more internal people being willing to expose their processes to scrutiny. Often such people have only the vaguest idea of what their problems actually are, but they sense that all is not as good as it could be and therefore invite observation and comment. The spirit of inquiry underlying this stance is an essential characteristic of a potentially successful client–consultant relationship.

The Exploratory Meeting

Who attends the exploratory meeting, where it is held, for what length of time, and whether or not the client will be billed for it has to be worked out jointly with the contact client. The PC philosophy requires that every intervention be jointly owned by the client system and the consultant, so the first work of the process consultant is to create a problem-solving process that will lead to a sound decision on the nature of the exploratory meeting.

The most important question is: Who should be present at such a meeting? If I have a chance to influence this decision, the kind of criteria that I use are as follows:

1. Someone high enough in the organization to be able to influence others if he is himself influenced.
2. Someone who is generally in tune with the idea of bringing in a consultant to work on organizational problems.

3. Someone who perceives a specific set of problems or symptoms that require attention.
4. Someone who is familiar with behavioral science consultants and the general notion that the client must remain active in the consultation process.

One should avoid having anyone at these early meetings who is hostile, skeptical, or totally ignorant of the kinds of service that can be offered by the consultant. If one or more such people are present and challenge me to prove that I can be of help to them, we are no longer exploring the problem. Instead I find myself seduced into a selling role, and if I permit myself to get into this role, I am already violating the PC model of helping others to help themselves. On the other hand, if the contact starts with members of the client system who are interested in trying PC, it is often possible at a later stage to design meetings or settings in which the resistant members of the system can be confronted constructively and conflicts worked through.

The exploratory meeting is usually a long lunch or a half day meeting. I usually mention to the contact client that the company should be prepared to pay a consultation fee for this meeting because the helping process really starts with the initial contact. The kinds of diagnostic questions I ask, the frame of reference from which I approach the problem, the sorts of things I observe and react to, all constitute initial interventions that, to some degree, influence the client's perceptions of his own problems. After three or four hours of exploration of his company's problems, the contact client has new perspective and new insights. At the same time I am sharing my scarcest resource — time.

The purposes of the exploratory meeting are as follows:

1. To determine more precisely what the problem is.
2. To assess whether my further involvement is likely to be of any help to the organization.
3. To assess whether the problem will be of interest to me.
4. To formulate next action steps with the client if the answers to 2 and 3 are positive.

The exploratory meeting is usually a fairly open-ended discussion during which I ask exploratory questions that are designed (1) to sharpen and highlight aspects of the presented problem, and (2) to test how open and frank the contact client is willing to be. If I feel that there is hedging, unwillingness to be critical of his own organization, confusion about his motives, and/or confusion about my potential role as a consultant, I am cautious. I suggest that nothing be decided without more exploration, or I terminate the relationship if I am definitely pessimistic about establishing a good relationship.

For example, in Case A the exploratory meeting was only with the contact client, a key manager immediately below the president. He spoke openly about his concerns that the president needed help in handling certain key people, shared his worries that the president and his key subordinates were not in good communication, and indicated that recent company history suggested the need for some stabilizing force in the organization. I asked him whether the president knew he had come to me and what the president's feelings were about bringing in a consultant. The contact client indicated that the president as well as other key executives were all in favor of bringing someone in to work with them. All saw the need for some outside help.

In Case B, the exploratory meeting was relatively perfunctory because I had already met the president at a management development session run by the company some months earlier. The meeting consisted of the personnel vice president, the president, and me, and moved rapidly toward the next stage of actually defining the goals and the setting in which to work.

In Case C, the fellow consultant who had recommended me acted as go-between and arranged a suitable set of goals and targets for my visit to the company. In Case D, the exploratory meeting was a lunch with the division manager, the inside consultant, and me. Our purpose was to determine whether the division manager and I would "hit it off together," whether we could agree on some reasonable goals for consultation, and how best to proceed if things looked promising.

In each of the above cases the initial exploration led to a

favorable response on both my part and that of the contact client. To illustrate an unfavorable outcome, in Case E, the Etna Production Company, the contact client called me to meet with him and his key personnel group to evaluate a new performance appraisal program they were planning to launch across the whole company. The contact client was the director of personnel. The exploratory meeting lasted for one day, during which time company representatives outlined the proposed program. I questioned a number of points that seemed internally inconsistent and found the client becoming obviously defensive. The further we went into the discussion, the clearer it became that the client was completely committed to his program and was seeking only reassurance from me. From the way in which he reacted to questions and criticisms, it also became clear that he was not willing to reexamine any part of his program. He did not really want an evaluation. I therefore terminated the relationship at the end of the day, saying that I did not think I could be helpful beyond the questions I had already raised.

I try to be as open and confronting as I can be during the exploratory meeting, partly as a test of how willing the client is to be open and partly to make it clear from the outset how I would define my role as consultant. The most important point to get across is that I will not function as an expert problem solver in the traditional consultant role. Rather, I will attempt to intervene directly in organizational processes as I see the opportunity. This point has to be made explicit early because the very entry of the consultant into the organization already constitutes an intervention of some magnitude. I would be deluding myself and my client if I said that I might or might not intervene, or that I would "study" the problem before intervening. I have to convince the client to accept the idea that intervention is fundamental to all stages of the consultation process, but that the nature and degree of intervention are dependent on joint diagnosis and joint decision making between the client and me.

If I feel that the contact client can accept me as an intervener in organizational processes, and if my relationship with the client is progressing comfortably during the exploratory meeting, the discussion usually moves toward defining the psychological contract.

The Psychological Contract

There are two aspects to the contract: (1) the formal decision as to how much time will be devoted to the consultation, what general services will be performed, and the form and amount of payment that will be used; and (2) the informal "psychological contract" that involves the client's implicit (and sometimes explicit) expectations of what he will gain from the relationship as well as what obligations he will accept, and the consultant's implicit (and sometimes explicit) expectations of what he will give to the relationship, what obligations he takes on, and what he expects to gain from it. It is important for both client and consultant to explore as many aspects of the contract as possible provided there is mutual understanding of what is meant. Sometimes this requires delaying the discussion until the client has experienced PC.

On the formal side, I have a simple ground rule. I work up to a certain number of days per month for a set per-hour and/or per-day fee. I do not wish the client organization to formally commit itself to a retainer or a predetermined contract of a given size, nor do I wish to promise a continuing relationship. Both parties should be free to terminate the agreement at any time if the relationship is no longer satisfactory or useful. This mutual freedom to terminate is important to ensure that the basis of the relationship is the *actual value obtained*, not the fulfillment of some obligation.

On the other hand, both the client and the consultant should be prepared to give as much time to the project as is mutually agreed on as desirable. If I have only one day per month available, and the nature of the problem is such that more time may be needed by the client, I obviously should not begin the consultation in the first place. I try to make a reasonably good estimate of how much time any given project might take if it goes well, and ensure that I have at least that much time available. For his part, the client should budget costs in such a way that if more days are needed, he has the resources to pay for them. In no case has anything of this sort ever been formalized beyond a general letter of intentions written by the client. Once we agree on the daily rate, I keep records of the amount of time spent and send monthly bills to the client.

On the psychological side, I try to assess as early in the relationship as possible all the expectations that may be deliberately or unwittingly concealed by the client. Beyond wanting to work on the presented problem, the client may expect the consultant to help in a variety of other ways, such as giving him personal evaluations of his subordinates, helping him deal with "problem people" in his organization, providing expert opinions on how certain management problems should be handled, giving support to some of the decisions the client has made, helping him to sell his decisions to others, serving as a communication channel to people with whom the client has trouble communicating, mediating conflicts, and so on. As many of these expectations as possible must be revealed early so that they do not become traps or sources of disappointment later if I refuse to go along with something that the client expects of me. On the other hand, if the client wishes to conceal certain motives, all I can do is to be diagnostically sensitive and avoid traps.

On my side, I have to be as clear as I can be about what I expect of the organization and of myself in my role as consultant. For example, I expect a willingness to diagnose and explore problem issues and to take enough time to find out what is really going on rather than rushing in hastily. I expect to be supported in my process orientation and to have organization members be committed to the process of sharing ownership of diagnostic and other interventions.

I also have to state clearly what I will do and what I will not do. For example, I have to explain fully the idea that my client is not just the *contact person* or the person of highest rank but the *entire group* with which I am working and, by implication, the entire organization. In other words, I would not support decisions that I believe would harm any given group, such as the employees, customers, or suppliers, even if I never had any contact with such groups.

This concept of the whole group or organization as the client is one of the trickiest, yet most important, aspects of PC. In observing other consultants operating in the organization in which I have been working, I have noticed that many of them essentially take the highest-level manager, typically the president, as their primary client, convince him of what the remedial intervention should be, and then proceed to help him to sell and implement the intervention even though this may be hurtful to others in the organization.

In contrast, as a process consultant, I have found myself to be most effective if I can gain the trust of *all* key parties with whom I am working so that none ever thinks of me as pushing someone else's ideas. I have found that this is quite possible to achieve across several levels of the organization. Indeed, in Case A, after many months of working with the president and his six key subordinates, I arrived at a point where all of them saw me as a potentially useful communication link. They asked me quite sincerely to report to each one the feelings or reactions of others whenever I learned anything that I felt should be passed on. At the same time they were quite open with me about each other, knowing that I might well pass on any opinions or reactions they voiced to me. They did not want me to treat everything they said to me as confidential, because they trusted me and each other enough and saw my linkage to all of them as an additional useful communication device.

This case was of great interest to me because of my own initial feelings that to serve as a carrier of this type of information was not an ideal role for me and reflected an insufficient ability on their part to tell each other things directly. Hence I took two courses of action. First, I tried as much as possible to train each of them to tell others in the group what they felt directly. At the same time, I intervened directly in their process by occasionally passing on information and opinions that they could not share when I thought this would be helpful in accomplishing their work goals.

A simple yet critical event will illustrate what I mean. Two members, Pete and Joe, did not always communicate freely with each other, partly because they felt some rivalry. Pete had completed a study and written a report that was to be discussed by the whole group. Three days before the report was due, I visited the company and stopped at Pete's office to discuss the report with him and ask how things were going. He said they were fine, but frankly he was puzzled about why Joe had not come to him to look at some of the back-up data pertaining to Joe's function. Pete felt this was just another bit of evidence that Joe did not really respect Pete very much.

An hour or so later I was working with Joe and raised the issue of the report (my unilateral decision to intervene because I thought it might be helpful). Joe and his staff were busy preparing for the meeting, but nothing was said about looking at the back-up data that Pete had available. Joe said that he was sure it was private and would not be released by Pete. Joe wanted badly to see it, but felt sure that Pete had deliberately not offered it.

I decided that it would be helpful to reveal what I knew about Pete's feelings of willingness to share the data. Joe expressed considerable surprise and later in the day went to Pete, who gave him a warm welcome and turned over to him three volumes of the data that Joe had been wanting to see and that Pete had been wanting to share. I had to judge carefully whether I would hurt either Pete or Joe by revealing Pete's feelings, and decided that the potential gains would clearly outweigh the risks.

Getting back to setting the proper expectations on the part of the client, I have to state clearly that I will not function as an expert resource on human relations problems, but that I will try to help the client to solve those problems by providing alternatives and helping to think through the consequences of different alternatives. I also need to stress my expectation that I will gather information primarily by observing people in action, not by interviewing and questionnaire surveying, unless there is a clear decision that interviewing a certain set of people is appropriate. Finally, I have to make it plain that when I am observing in meetings, I will not be very active but will comment on what is happening or give feedback only as I feel it will be helpful to the group in accomplishing its task.

The fact that I will be relatively inactive is often a problem for the group because of their expectation that once they have hired a consultant they are entitled to sit back and just listen to him tell them things. To have the consultant then spend hours sitting in the group and saying very little not only violates this expectation but also creates some anxiety about what he is observing. The more I can reassure the group early in the game that I am not gathering personal data of a potentially damaging nature, the smoother the subsequent observations will go.

Summary

All consultations start with some contact client who gets in touch with the consultant. Together they work out the next step, which often is an exploratory meeting that will involve others from the client organization. During such a meeting one begins to spell out mutual expectations.

Part of the early exploration with the contact client and any associates whom he involves is intended to establish a clear psychological contract that will govern the ongoing consultation. As I have indicated, I feel there should not be a formal contract beyond an agreement on fees and the potential number of days to be committed at the outset. Each party should be free to terminate or change this level of involvement at any time. At the level of the psychological contract it is important to get out into the open as many misconceptions as possible and to try to be as clear as possible about my own aims and style of work.

11

Settings and Methods of Work

The final issue to be addressed in the exploratory meeting or in subsequent meetings involves the selection of a setting in which to work, the specification of a time schedule, a description of the method of work to be used, and a preliminary statement about goals to be achieved. These decisions are crucial because, by implication, they define the immediate client system to which the consultant will relate himself.

The Setting

I use a number of general criteria for making decisions about the setting:

1. *The choice of what and when to observe should be worked out collaboratively with the client.* The process consultant must avoid the image of a psychologist wandering around the organization making observations about anything that strikes him as needing attention. Instead, the consultant should engage in a focused process of observation and feedback where both par-

ticipant and observer have agreed to inquire into the problem-solving process for the sake of improving it.

If the consultant feels the locus of observation should shift, he must involve the people who work in this new locus and establish a similar contract with them. Since the participants are themselves the targets of the process interventions, it is essential that they be involved in the decision to try to learn. Without this kind of psychological contract there is at best no readiness to hear what the consultant might have to say and at worst real resentment at being observed by an outsider.

2. *The setting chosen should be as near the top of the organization or client system as possible.* The reasons for beginning observations at the highest possible level are twofold. First, the higher the level, the more likely that basic norms, values, and goals can be observed in operation. The higher levels set the tone of the organization and ultimately determine the criteria for effective organizational functioning. If the consultant does not expose himself to these levels, he cannot determine what these ultimate norms, goals, and criteria are, and if he does not become acquainted with them, he is abdicating his own ethical responsibility.

Only if the consultant can personally accept the norms, goals, and criteria of the organization can he justify helping the organization to achieve them. If the consultant feels that the organization's goals are unethical, immoral, or personally unacceptable for some other reason, he can choose to attempt to change them or terminate the relationship, but this choice should be made. The consultant should not operate in ignorance of what the established authority in the organization is trying to do.

Second, the higher the level, the greater the payoff on any changes in process that are achieved. In other words, if the consultant can help the president to learn more about organizational process and to change his behavior accordingly, this change in turn is a force on his immediate subordinates which sets a chain of influence into motion. The more general way to put this point is to say that the consultant should seek that setting or group of people that he considers to be potentially most influential on the rest of the organization. Usually this turns out to be the top executive group.

3. *The setting chosen should be one in which it is easy to observe problem-solving, interpersonal, and group processes.* Often this turns out to be a weekly or monthly staff meeting, or some other regularly scheduled activity in which two or more members of the key group being observed transact business together. It is important to observe processes among the members, not just between individual members and the consultant. For this reason, a survey or interview methodology is only a stopgap measure. Ultimately, the consultant must have access to a situation where the organization's members are dealing with each other in their usual fashion.

4. *The setting chosen should be one in which real work is going on.* The consultant should avoid the situation where a group initially agrees to meet with him only to discuss their interpersonal relations. Such a meeting would be appropriate after a relationship had developed between the group and the consultant but would be premature before. The group cannot as yet trust the consultant enough to really have an open discussion of interpersonal relations, and the consultant does not yet have enough observational data to be able to help the group in such a discussion. Regular committee or work-group meetings are ideal, on the other hand, because the consultant not only sees the organization members in a more natural role but learns what sort of work the members are concerned about. At later stages, it is much easier to link observations to real work behavior, and it is much more likely that real changes will occur in members if they can relate process observations to work events.

These criteria can often not be met in an absolute fashion, but they are an important guideline. If the criteria are shared with the contact client in the process of getting joint ownership of the decision on setting, the consultant is also beginning to intervene by teaching the client something about the process of planned change.

Method of Work

The method of work chosen should be as congruent as possible with the values underlying process consultation. Thus observation, informal interviewing, and group discussions would be congruent with (a) the idea that the consultant does not already have pat answers or standard "expert" solutions, and (b) the idea that the consultant should be maximally available for questioning and two-way communication.

If the consultant uses such methods as questionnaires or surveys, he himself remains an unknown quantity to the respondent. As long as he remains unknown, the respondent cannot really trust him and hence cannot answer questions completely honestly. The method of work chosen, therefore, should make the consultant maximally visible and maximally available for interaction.

Often I choose to start a consultation project with some interviewing, but the purpose of the interview is not so much to gather data as to establish a relationship with each of the people who will later be observed. The interview is designed to reveal myself as much as to learn something about the other person. I consider the use of questionnaires only after I am well enough known by the organization to be reasonably sure that people would trust me enough to give direct and frank answers to questions.

In the Apex Manufacturing Company, the exploratory meeting led to the decision to attend one of the regular meetings of the executive committee. At this time I was to meet the president and the other key executives to discuss further what could and should be done. At the meeting I found a lively interest in the idea of having an outsider help the group and the organization to become more effective. I also found that the group was willing to enter an open-ended relationship. I explained as much as I could my philosophy of PC and suggested that a good way of getting further acquainted would be to set up a series of individual interviews with each member of the group. At the same time I suggested that I sit in on the weekly half-day meetings of the executive committee. The interviews then would occur after several of these meetings.

At the initial meeting of the group, I was able to observe a number of key events. For example, the president, Alex, was very informal but very powerful. I got the impression initially (and confirmed it subsequently) that the relationships of all the group members to the president would be the key issue, with relationships to each other being relatively less important. I also got the impression that Alex was a confident individual who would tolerate my presence only so long as he saw some value in it; he would have little difficulty in confronting me and terminating the relationship if my presence ceased to have value.

It was also impressive, and turned out to be indicative of a managerial style, that Alex did not feel the need to see me alone. He was satisfied from the outset to deal with me inside the group. Near the end of the initial meeting, I requested a private talk with him to satisfy myself that we understood the psychological contract we were entering into. He was surprisingly uncomfortable in this one-to-one relationship, had little that he wished to impart to me, and did not show much interest in my view of the relationship. I wanted the private conversation in order to test his reaction to taking some personal feedback on his own behavior as the consultation progressed. He said he would welcome this and indicated little or no concern over it. As I was to learn later, his reaction reflected a very strong sense of his own power and identity. He felt he knew himself very well and was not a bit threatened by feedback.

In the Boyd Consumer Goods Company, the consultation started in essentially the same manner. At the exploratory meeting with the president, Bill, I inquired whether there was some regular meeting that he held with his immediate subordinates. There was such a group that met weekly, and it was agreed that I would sit in on it. Bill explained to the group that he had asked me to sit in to help the group function more effectively and then asked me to explain how I saw my own role. I described PC and the kinds of things I would be looking for, stated that I would not be very active but preferred the group just to work along as it normally would, and that I would make comments as I saw opportunities to be helpful. It was decided that after a few meetings I would interview each member of the seven-man group individually.

The climate of the Boyd group was quite formal. There was not much group participation, more reliance on Bill to run the meeting, and more ambiguity about the feelings of the members for each other.

In the Central Chemical Company the pattern was entirely different, since they were geographically removed and I had contracted to spend only one week with them at a time several months hence. The person coordinating my program was quite knowledgeable about the possible uses he could make of a process consultant, and he had, as I indicated before, consulted with a colleague of mine to determine how best to use me. They decided that a workshop devoted to helping line managers improve their diagnoses and action plans for change programs that they wanted to implement was an appropriate workshop goal. Once this had been decided by correspondence, I worked with my colleague on designing the program of the week. We agreed not to freeze the plan until I was actually on the premises the evening before the workshop. We had, however, made the key decision to invite only managers who had an interest in changing some aspect of their immediate work situation, and to have each manager come with a member of the personnel staff reporting to him so that teams would be looking at the change problems.

When I arrived at the Central Chemical Company site some months later, I met with my "inside" consultant contact, his boss (who was personnel director), and one or two other personnel people who were interested in the program. We reviewed the goals and schedule of the week, decided to remain flexible until we could find out more from the participants about their change goals, and agreed that the inside consultant would work with me in implementing the program. The setting for the program was the training center of the company. All the teams (eighteen men altogether) were to meet daily at the training center for the actual workshop.

In the case of Delta, the pattern was almost identical to Apex and Boyd. The head of the division with whom I had the exploratory lunch (Dave) decided that he wanted to build his group of immediate subordinates into an effective team so that they could manage what he saw as a difficult phase involving the rapid growth of the division. He held weekly staff meetings and invited me to sit in on these regularly. After several meetings, I planned, as in the other cases, to interview each member of the seven-person group individually.

To illustrate a different kind of setting and work method, let us look at the Fairview Company. Some members of the training department had become exposed to sensitivity training several years back, introduced it into their middle and senior manager development programs, and gained a good deal of sophistication in analyzing organizational process. It became clear to a number of them that one of the major difficulties of the organization was conflict between the central headquarters and the various field units — conflicts over how much decentralization of decision-making authority there should be, conflicts concerning how much the system actually reflected earlier agreements to decentralize, and conflicts over lines of authority.

The organization had strong functional directors in the headquarters organization. As they developed financial and marketing programs, they tended to bypass the formal line organization through the executive vice president and the regional managers, instead dealing directly with the financial and marketing people in the field.

The central training group knew that there was an annual meeting of all the key executives, including headquarters and field people — fifteen in all. They consulted me about the possibility of organizing one of these meetings in such a way as to enable the entire group to work on the organizational problem. The training group was not sure how the president or vice president would respond to the idea, since there was no prior history of exposure of the group to an outside consultant. However, a number of the regional managers had attended sensitivity training groups and learned something about the potential of bringing in a "behaviorally oriented consultant." They felt strongly that something like this meeting should be tried.

A core group, consisting of the training director, two of his key staff people, and one enthusiastic regional manager, met with me for one day to plan further strategy. We decided that for such a program to work, a substantial number of the people who would eventually be at the meeting would also have to become involved in the planning and design of the meeting. This step was a crucial one, and can be derived directly from the kind of assumptions that underlie PC. A group consisting of equal numbers of head-quarters and regional managers was formed. The mission of this group was to meet for two days to plan the total meeting. The plan developed by the group was then to be presented for approval to the president and vice president.

My role as a process consultant was critical at two stages in this enterprise. First, during the two-day meeting of the planning group I had to steer them away from a traditional format in which I would make presentations about headquarters/field-type problems for them to discuss. Second, I had to take responsibility for the success of the meeting format finally chosen and find a role for myself that would make this format work.

The plan that emerged from the two days of planning had the following elements:

1. The three-day meeting would be billed as an exploration of organizational problems at the top of the organization, toward the end of improving organizational relationships.
2. The meeting would be chaired by me rather than the president of the company.
3. The agenda for the meeting would be developed by a procedure used by Richard Beckhard in which each member of the fifteen-person group would be asked to write me a letter at my home outlining what he saw to be the major organizational problems facing the group. It was then my job to put together the information from the fifteen letters into major themes and issues. These themes and issues were to be presented by me to the total group at our first session and could constitute the agenda for the three days.

The first purpose in having such letters written was to provide each person the opportunity to be completely frank without having to expose himself to the possible wrath of the boss or other members of the group. Second, it provided an opportunity to gather data from all the members before the meeting began.

Third, it involved each member in helping to set the agenda, a considerable departure from previous meetings where the agenda had been set by the vice president. It could be expected, therefore, that all the members would feel more involved in the meeting from the outset.

The letter writing had two problems connected with it: (1) it seemed a little bit gimmicky, and (2) it was difficult to know how someone would react who had not as yet met me. Would he write a frank letter to a strange professor about rather critical organizational issues? We decided that we would have to run the risk of getting no response or poor response, but that we could minimize the risk by having the members of the planning group talk to others they knew and make a personal appeal to write a frank letter.

The procedure was agreed on, was presented to the president and vice president and received enthusiastic approval, and thus became the plan for the meeting. I pointed out that the president and vice president would have to be careful in how they managed their own role. If they reverted too quickly to their power position and abandoned the role of helping to diagnose organizational problems, the group would retreat into silence and the problems would remain unsolved. I felt that both men understood the risks, were willing to take them, and had the kind of personality that would make them accept this somewhat strange meeting format.

Having agreed to go ahead, the group then decided that the vice president would send out the letter explaining the meeting format and inviting the diagnostic letters. Members of the planning group were to follow up in the districts to ensure that everyone understood the plan and the fact that the plan had come from organization members themselves, even though I had suggested many of the separate elements.

This rather lengthy procedure was essential to obtain the involvement of the members in a process-oriented meeting. Even though the ideas came from the training department and from me, the concept clearly appealed to regional and headquarters managers. Had they not become committed, it would not have been possible to hold such a meeting at all.

Summary

The choice of a setting and a method of work is highly variable. It is important that both the setting and working procedure be jointly decided between the contact client group and the consultant. Whatever decisions are made should be congruent with the general assumptions underlying PC so that whatever changes result can be self-perpetuating.

12

Diagnostic Interventions

Once the consultant is attending meetings, observing work, interviewing people, and otherwise becoming part of the ongoing organizational scene, he is engaged in a whole stream of activities that can best be conceptualized as two types of interventions — *diagnostic* and *confrontive*. In this chapter I will analyze what I mean by a diagnostic intervention and in the next two chapters take up the concept of confrontive intervention.

Gathering Data Through Diagnostic Interventions

Every decision to observe something, to ask a question, or to meet with someone constitutes an intervention into the ongoing organizational process. The consultant cannot, therefore, avoid or escape taking the responsibility for the kind of data-gathering method he uses. If the method is not congruent with his overall values, and if it does not meet the standards for an acceptable intervention, it should not be used.

The point is worth belaboring because all of the traditional consultation models, as well as the models of how to do research on organizations, make the glib assumption that one gathers data *prior* to intervening; that one observes, interviews, and surveys, then makes a diagnosis, and then suggests interventions or remedial steps.

From the point of view of PC this is an inaccurate and dangerous assumption. It is inaccurate because one can clearly demonstrate that the process of being studied influences the parties being studied. If I interview someone about his organization, the very questions I ask give the respondent ideas he never had before. The very process of formulating his own answers gives him points of view that he may never have thought of before.

The assumption is also dangerous because the various respondents who have been interviewed, surveyed, or studied may, by virtue of this common experience, band together and decide on their own what kind of action they would like to see. While the researcher-consultant is off analyzing his data, the respondents are busy changing the organization or generating demands that their boss may be quite unprepared for.

What, then, is the correct assumption, and what are its implications? The correct assumption is that every act on the part of the process consultant — even the initial act of deciding to work with the organization — constitutes an intervention. Asking for help, and having someone accept some responsibility for helping, changes the perceptions and attitudes of some members of the organization. The consultant cannot ignore these changes. He must anticipate them and learn to make them work toward the ultimate goals defined.

The main implication of this latter assumption is that the consultant must think through everything he does in terms of its probable impact on the organization. He must assume that all of his behavior is an intervention of one sort or another. Finally, he must use data-gathering methods that, at the same time, will constitute valid and useful interventions.

Methods of Data Gathering

Basically, the consultant has only three different methods by which he can gather data:

1. Direct observation
2. Individual or group interviews
3. Questionnaires or some other survey instrument to be filled out

I have already indicated that the third method is too impersonal and too much at variance with PC assumptions to be useful in the early stages of a PC project. It may become useful if the number of people to be surveyed is rather large and if the managers with whom the consultant is working fully understand the implications involved in taking a survey.

For early data gathering the choice is then reduced to observation and/or interview. In my own experience I have found that a combination of these techniques is optimal. I need a certain amount of observation in order to know what kinds of issues should be brought up in interviews, but I need some preliminary interviews in order to know whom and what to observe.

These criteria usually lead to a top-down kind of strategy. I start with the data provided by the contact client. The exploratory meeting is usually an opportunity to gather data in a group-interview setting. As the examples above have shown, the next step is often an interview of one or more of the senior people who will be involved in the project. Their consent must be obtained to do any observation of them in interaction with their group. Regular group members are usually interviewed only after one or two meetings during which I have observed what kinds of issues are being discussed and what kinds of problems exist within the group.

Once a relationship has been formed with some key group in the organization, new projects develop that involve new settings, but the methods of gathering data in the new settings are essentially the same. For example, one of the managers of the original group may want to know how the members of his own staff group feel about the organization and the work setting. He and I may then plan a series of interviews of his subordinates, leading to a series of feedback meetings. This procedure will not be initiated, however, until the manager has obtained the support and consent of his subordinates and until they too feel that I can be trusted. If it is not convenient for me to meet all of them and/ or observe their meetings, a relatively greater burden falls on the manager to persuade his subordinates to participate. But the project cannot proceed until the subordinates genuinely agree.

In this connection, an important criterion for extending a data-gathering method is that the manager who would like to use it should himself have participated in an earlier project. If the manager has been interviewed by me and has heard what kind of feedback I give after a series of interviews, he is in a much better position to decide whether such a technique would be useful in his group, and he is better equipped to explain to his subordinates what the procedure will be like.

No data-gathering method is right or wrong in the abstract. Whether or not it is appropriate and useful can be judged only from earlier observations and interviews. In a way the entire PC project must always be viewed as an unfolding series of events where subsequent events can only be predicted from earlier events. The project should be planned in a general way, but the issues that come up in the flow of work, and the new behaviors that are generated by the earlier interventions, are hard to predict, and some of the most important ones are those for which the least planning was done.

What should be the content of interviews or surveys? I have discussed in Part II of this book the kinds of things the consultant looks for when he observes a group in action. These general categories of organizational and interpersonal process should always be on the consultant's mind as things to be sensitive to, but I have found that to ask directly about them is not useful. Instead what should guide an interview or survey is the presented problem and the goals of the consultation.

For example, in the Apex Manufacturing Company, part of the initial mandate was to help the group to relate to the president. In the interviews that I conducted with group members, I concentrated quite heavily on what kinds of things went well in the relationship, what kinds of things went poorly, how relationship problems with the president were related to job performance, in what way the group members would like to see the relationship change, and so on. I did not have a formal interview schedule but held an informal discussion with each member around issues of the sort I have just mentioned.

In contrast, when I began to interview group members in the Boyd and Central companies, I concentrated much more on what kind of job each member had, with whom he had to work in the performance of that job, what kinds of problems existed in any of these relationships, what organizational factors aided or hindered effective job performance, what the company climate was like, and so on.

In the case of the Delta Manufacturing Company, I gathered no data until the evening before the workshop, and subsequently within the workshop itself. In the Fairview Company, on the other hand, I gathered written data by means of the letters. In this case, each respondent was invited to write down whatever he saw as problems existing in the relationships between the headquarters organization and the various regional centers.

The common theme in all these data-gathering approaches is a concern with organizational relationships and perceptions of organizational processes. The specific questions vary, but the general area is the same. The other common thread is a concern with organizational effectiveness. I always attempt to determine what factors are helping to make the person, group, or unit more effective, and what factors are undermining or hindering effectiveness. My assumption is that both sets of factors are always present in any organization.

Intervention Style

Having identified the kinds of content areas that I explore in interviews, I would like to close the discussion by describing some of the aspects of style, or how the consultant presents himself. For example, in the interview itself, my method of asking questions and the content of what I ask project a certain image of me. If I want to establish a collaborative, helping relationship with the person being interviewed, I must behave in a manner congruent with such a relationship. This means I cannot play the role of the psychologist who asks obscure questions upon which I then place "secret" interpretations or the like.

The content of the questions should be self-evidently relevant. If I am concerned about improving organizational effectiveness, then I should ask about it. If I am concerned with improvement, I should ask about those things that are going well in addition to those which are going poorly.

The questions can push the respondent into areas he might not ordinarily think to mention, provided that they are relevant and that the consultant senses a willingness on the part of the respondent to enter into those areas. For example, in all of the cases mentioned, I asked quite probing questions about how the decision was made to use a consultant, the attitudes expressed by members toward my coming in, what they thought were my particular qualifications for the job, where there might be tension over having a consultant in, and so on. As I mentioned earlier, if the contact client is unwilling to deal with these areas openly in the early discussions, I am likely to be cautious about becoming involved. Once working within the organization, I would interpret unwillingness to deal with such areas as caution on the respondent's part, and it would be up to me to try to determine the reasons for the caution.

The kind of question one asks also puts new ideas into the head of the respondent. For example, I often ask what kind of career planning a person has engaged in with others in the organization. The answer often is "None," but a new issue often comes up later in the interview in the form of "I wonder why no one has sat down with me to talk about my career," or "Maybe I should go have a talk with my boss about my future in the company." If I ask a person to describe the network of others with whom he must deal in order to get his job done, he often realizes for the first time what this network is like and why he has problems keeping up with his job. In other words, the interview can be a powerful tool of influence and education, and the process consultant must consider when and how to use it for influence purposes.

If I have reason to believe that the interviewee may be defensive or want to present a socially desirable picture, I ask factual and historical questions. Direct questions about values or opinions are the most likely to come back biased and thus are typically avoided.

Summary

There are basically three kinds of data-gathering methods: observation, interview, and questionnaire. Because any one of the methods is some kind of intervention into organizational process, the consultant must choose a method that will be most congruent with the values underlying PC and with the general goals of the PC project. The way he gathers data and the kinds of questions he asks give the consultant an opportunity to intervene constructively. In the next chapter I will take a closer look at other kinds of intervention to explore more fully the options available to the consultant.

13

Influencing Process Through Confrontive Interventions: Agenda Management

Deliberately Altering Process
Through Confrontive Intervention

Deliberately Altering Process
Through Confrontive Intervention

As I have shown, one cannot completely separate the stages of diagnostic data gathering and intervention. Both occur simultaneously: how one gathers data constitutes an intervention, and the kind of intervention one chooses will reveal new data derived from the reaction to the intervention. The separation of these two processes is, therefore, basically a matter of point of view or frame of reference. In the last chapter I focused on those interventions that are primarily designed to elicit diagnostic information. In this and the next chapter I will focus on interventions that are specific attempts to change organizational process by deliberate actions on the part of the consultant.

The interventions that a process consultant might make cannot be rigidly classified, but a broad categorization can be suggested:

A. Agenda-managing interventions
    1. Questions that direct attention to process issues

2. Process-analysis periods
3. Meetings devoted to process issues
4. Conceptual inputs on process-related topics

B. Feedback of observations or other data
   1. Feedback to groups during process analysis or regular work time
   2. Feedback to individuals after meetings or after data gathering

C. Coaching or counseling of individuals or groups

D. Structural suggestions
   1. Pertaining to group membership
   2. Pertaining to communication or interaction patterns
   3. Pertaining to allocation of work, assignment of responsibility, and lines of authority

The outline is arranged in terms of a descending likelihood of use of the particular intervention. In other words, the kind of intervention I am most likely to make pertains to the group's agenda; the kind I am least likely to make is a structural suggestion. Actual solutions to management problems are not even listed because they would not be considered valid interventions in a PC model. If I permitted myself to become interested in a particular management problem in sales, marketing, or production, I would be switching roles from that of process consultant to that of expert resource. Once I have become an expert resource, I find I lose my effectiveness as a process consultant.

Agenda-Managing Interventions

Process-oriented Questions and Process-Analysis Periods

The basic purpose of this type of intervention is to make the group sensitive to its own internal processes, and to generate on the part of the group some interest in analyzing these processes. In the early stages of a project, I often find myself suggesting to a group that they allocate fifteen minutes or so at the end of their meeting to review the meeting. I may suggest some dimensions such as how involved they felt, how clear communications were, how well member resources were used, and so on. If the group is willing, I have them fill in a postmeeting reaction form (see pp. 57–58) and tabulate their own data for further discussion. If the group agrees to some period of time for process analysis, no matter how short, I can further stimulate their interest by asking them questions that direct their attention to process issues. In addition, I will usually have observed particular events that have been important during the meeting.

For example, in a number of meetings I have observed the chairman making decisions hastily and without full commitment from the group. My question during a process-review period then might be: "How did you all feel about how the decision was made?" I have to resist answering the question with my own feelings. First of all, my feelings might be irrelevant or atypical; and second, I want the group to learn to gather its own data and draw its own conclusions. If I am pressed, I will answer with my observation or my own feeling, but my preference is usually to turn the question back to the group.

Out of process-analysis sessions there often arise two further issues, leading to further interventions. The group sometimes discovers that it has a variety of dissatisfactions with the manner in which it arrives at and processes its work agenda. I find myself at this point suggesting various ways by which the group can evaluate what to put on the agenda, how much time to allocate to each item, how to sort items in terms of importance or type of problem, and so on.

The other issue pertains to the matter of interpersonal process itself. The more interested the group becomes in its own workings, the more time it devotes to discussing this topic and the less time there is for its regular agenda. To deal with this dilemma I often suggest that process work could perhaps be done in depth by periodically allocating a whole meeting or some set block of time just to processes in the group.

Meetings Devoted to Process Issues

Such meetings are often held away from the office at a motel or some other detached location to permit the group to really work on group issues. I do not suggest this kind of meeting, however, until I believe the group is emotionally ready to handle a larger dose of process analysis. One of the frequent mistakes I have observed in colleagues' efforts to help organizations is an initial suggestion of holding a meeting to explore "relationships" and "interpersonal issues." Such a meeting should not be scheduled without firsthand knowledge that members want it and are ready to deal emotionally with whatever issues might come up.

Conceptual Inputs

The final subheading under agenda-managing interventions concerns the matter of presenting relevant elements of theory about individuals, groups, and management process. I do not have a set pattern of what I offer a group or when I offer it, but some examples may make clear the use of this intervention.

In the Apex Manufacturing Company, I found that the treasurer consistently made the operating managers uncomfortable by presenting financial information in an unintentionally threatening way. He wanted to be helpful, and he felt everyone needed the information he had to offer, but it often had the appearance of an indictment of one of the other managers: his costs were too high, his inventory control had slipped, he was too high over budget, and so on. Furthermore, this information was often revealed for the first time in the meeting, so that the operating manager concerned had no forewarning and no opportunity to find out why things had gone out of line. The result was often a fruitless argument about the validity of the figures, a great deal of defensiveness on the part of the operating manager, and irritation on the part of the president because the managers could not deal more effectively with the treasurer.

As I observed this process occurring repeatedly over several weeks, I decided that merely drawing attention to the pattern would not really solve the problem because everyone appeared to be operating with constructive intent. What the group needed was an alternative way to think about the use of financial control information. I therefore wrote a memo (see Appendix A) on control systems and circulated it to the group. When this came up for discussion at a later meeting I was in a better position to make my observations about the group, since a clear alternative had been presented. My feeling was that I could not have successfully presented this theory orally because of the amount of heat the issue always generated, and because the group members were highly active individuals who would have wanted to discuss each point separately, making it difficult to get the whole message across.

In working with the Apex group I found the written "theory memo" a convenient and effective means of communication (see samples in the Appendix). With other groups I found different patterns to be workable. For example, if the group gets away for a half day of work on group process, I may insert a half hour in the middle (or at the end) of the session to present whatever theory elements I consider to be relevant. The topics are usually not selected until I observe the particular "hangups" that exist in the group. I therefore have to be prepared to offer, on short notice, input on any of a variety of issues.

A final method of theory input is to make reprints of relevant articles available to the group at selected times. Often I know of some good piece of theory that pertains to what the group is working on. If I suggest that such an article be circulated, I also try to persuade the group to commit some of its agenda time to a discussion of the article.

The key criterion for the choice of theory input is that the theory must be relevant to what the group already senses is a problem. There is little to be gained by giving "important" theory if the group has no data of its own to link to the theory. On the other hand, once the group has confronted an issue in its own process, I am always amazed at how ready the members are to look at and learn from general theory.

Agenda-managing interventions may strike the reader as a rather low-key, low-potency kind of intervention. Yet it is surprising to me how often working groups arrive at an impasse on simple agenda-managing issues. In a way, their inability to select the right agenda for their meetings and to discuss the agenda in a constructive way is symbolic of other difficulties that are harder to pinpoint. If the group can begin to work on its agenda, the door is often opened to other process discussions. Let me provide some case examples.

Case Examples

In the Apex Manufacturing Company I sat in for several months on the weekly executive committee meeting, which included the president and his key subordinates. I quickly became aware that the group was very loose in its manner of operation: people spoke when they felt like it, issues were explored fully, conflict was confronted fairly openly, and members felt free to contribute.

This kind of climate seemed constructive, but it created a major difficulty for the group. No matter how few items were put on the agenda, the group was never able to finish its work. The list of backlog items grew longer and the frustration of group members intensified in proportion to this backlog. The group resonded by trying to work harder. They scheduled more meetings and attempted to get more done at each meeting, but with little success. Remarks about the ineffectiveness of groups, too many meetings, and so on became more and more frequent.

The group was obviously overloaded but did not know how to cope with this condition. Their agenda was too large, they tried to process too many items at any given meeting, and the agenda was a mixture of operational and policy issues without recognition by the group that such items required different allocations of time. I suggested to the group that they seemed overloaded and should discuss how to develop their agenda for their meetings. The suggestion was adopted after a half hour or so of sharing feelings. It was then decided, with my help, to sort the agenda items into several categories, and to devote some meetings entirely to operational issues while others would be exclusively policy meetings. The operations meetings would be run more tightly in order to process these items efficiently. The policy questions would be dealt with in depth.

Once the group had made this separation and realized that it could function differently at different meetings, it then decided to meet once a month for an entire day. During this day they would take up one or two large questions and explore them in depth. The group accepted my suggestion to hold such discussions away from the office in a pleasant, less hectic environment.

By rearranging the agenda, the group succeeded in rearranging its whole pattern of operations. This rearrangement also resulted in a redefinition of my role. The president decided that I should phase out my attendance at the operational meetings but plan to take a more active role in the monthly one-day meetings. He would set time aside for presentation of any theory I might wish to make and for process analysis of the meetings. He had previously been reluctant to take time for process work in the earlier meeting pattern but now welcomed it.

The full-day meetings changed the climate of the group dramatically. For one thing, it was easier to establish close informal relationships with other members during breaks and meals. Because there was enough time, people felt they could really work through their conflicts instead of having to leave them hanging. It was my impression that as acquaintance level rose, so did the level of trust in the group. Members began to feel free to share more personal reactions with each other. This sense of freedom made everyone more relaxed and readier to let down personal barriers and report accurate information. There was less need for defensive distortion or withholding.

After about one year the group decided quite spontaneously to try some direct confrontive feedback. We were at one of the typical monthly all-day meetings. The president announced that he thought each group member should tell the others what he felt to be the strengths and weaknesses of the several individuals. He asked me to help in designing a format for this discussion. I first asked the group members whether they did in fact want to attempt this type of confrontation. The response was sincerely positive, so we decided to go ahead.

The format I suggested was based upon my prior observation of group members. I had noticed that whenever anyone commented on anyone else, there was a strong tendency to answer back and to lock in on the first comment made. Hence, further feedback tended to be cut off. To deal with this problem I suggested that the group discuss one person at a time, and that a ground rule be established that the person being described was not to comment or respond until all the members had had a chance to give all of their feedback. This way he would be forced to continue to listen. The ground rule was accepted, and I was given the role of monitoring the group to ensure that the process operated as the group intended it to.

For the next several hours the group then went into a detailed and searching analysis of each member's managerial and interpersonal style, including that of the president. I encouraged members to discuss both the positives and the negatives they saw in each person. I also played a key role in forcing people to make their comments specific and concrete. I demanded examples, insisted on clarification, and generally asked the kind of question that I thought might be on the listener's mind as he tried to understand the feedback. I also added my own feedback on points I had observed in that member's behavior.

At first it was not easy for the group either to give or to receive feedback, but as the day wore on the group learned to be more effective. The total exercise of confrontation was considered highly successful, both at the time and some months later. It deepened relationships, exposed some chronic problems that now could be worked on, and gave each member much food for thought in terms of his own self-development. It should be noted that the group chose to do this spontaneously after many months of meetings organized around work topics. I am not sure they could have handled the feedback task effectively had they been urged to try sooner, even though I could see the need for this type of meeting some time before the initiative came from the group.

In the Apex case, my intervention tended to help the group move from chaotic meetings toward a differentiated, organized pattern. In the end, the group spent more time in meetings than before, but they minded it less because the meetings were more productive. The group has also learned how to manage its own agenda and how to guide its own processes.

In the Boyd Consumer Goods Company, a similar situation was present but the direction of learning was different. I found that the executive group was strangling itself with formality and trivia. Agendas were long and detailed, meetings were highly formal, and members were responsible for reporting to the group on various operational issues on a carefully planned monthly schedule. If anyone tried to make comments on a report, he was quickly reminded that he knew less about the topic than the reporter. Consequently most of the talk during meetings was of a reporting, attack, or defense variety. Little open-ended problem solving took place. Most members looked (and acted) passive and bored. When interviewed, they confirmed that they felt this way during meetings; yet, surprisingly, they tended to defend their meetings as necessary.

My own feeling was that the members were caught up in their own traditions. They had always run meetings this way; hence they felt that boredom and lack of involvement were the "normal" subjective feelings for participants in a meeting. Those who felt a little more frustrated and rebellious did not know what methods to follow for livelier, more productive meetings. Hence there were widespread feelings of apathy, resignation, and frustration.

I tried a whole series of interventions over a period of several months, most of them unsuccessful from my point of view. First, I asked the group to review its own agenda and share feelings about it. Some members revealed feelings of frustration but still staunchly defended the agenda pattern as necessary. Second, I tried to help the group to differentiate policy from operational decisions. It seemed to me that whenever they tried to discuss policy, operational problems would intervene and preempt a major portion of the time. I also felt that the group tended to hold too limited a concept of policy. The group verbally agreed with me but failed to change its pattern of operation in any substantial way. Third, I tried being directly confrontive about the apathy and frustration I saw in the members. The group accepted my confrontation like "good soldiers," defended itself a little bit, told me I had been very helpful, and then resumed its discussions in the old pattern.

A partial breakthrough came some months later. The president of the company had in the meantime attended a sensitivity-training lab and had come back with a somewhat greater enthusiasm for group-process work. He realized that the group could be more productive and recognized the need to make it so. We agreed to devote some time to discussion of what the group's agenda and pattern of operations should be. In the meantime, another event had taken place: the company had reorganized, putting responsibility for many of the day-to-day operational problems clearly on the shoulders of certain key individuals. To make the reorganization work, it was decided not to have as much group time devoted to reporting out and monitoring members' work areas.

When the group met to discuss its own future, some of the same depression I had previously observed was still in evidence. After about twenty minutes of general discussion, I said in a rather exasperated tone that I never saw this group have any *fun*. What would it take to make people want to come to the meeting because the meeting would be *fun*? This comment released a burst of laughter, as if some kind of inner dam had burst. The group had really been operating on the assumption that work could not be fun, and was just silently taking its painful medicine.

Once this issue had been brought out into the open, members agreed that meetings could be more fun. In the subsequent discussion, members delineated several key requirements for better meetings: a climate of greater acceptance in the group which would permit members to share ideas, plans, and problems with each other, without feeling that they would be attacked by other members; more concentration on sharing information and problems, and less on trying to make decisions in the group; and more effective use of group time by better agenda control.

The group spent an hour or more discussing how it might operate in the future and, more important, agreed on the use of a process-analysis session at the end of each meeting, to review whether it was hitting its own targets. It was decided that one member of the group should be the process recorder and give feedback to the group at the end of the session. This decision was especially good since the members needed practice in observing group process. Shortly afterward, my participation in the meetings was curtailed by other commitments, but at a later time I had an opportunity to discuss the group's progress with the president, and he felt that the meetings improved, that the climate became more open, and that the process-observer role has been very helpful to the group in monitoring its own functioning.

This case illustrates for me the trial-and-error nature of intervention. I could not really have predicted which of my various efforts to loosen the group up would work. Indeed, if there had not been related changes, such as the reorganization and the president's experience at the training laboratory, maybe none of my efforts would have worked. Merely helping the group to identify its process does not automatically produce a change in that process, even if the group is quite frustrated and knows a change is needed.

Summary and Analysis

Agenda-managing interventions are one category of confrontive interventions that are designed to deliberately influence the group's process. Such interventions are confrontive because they draw the client's attention to process issues that cannot be evaded. Everyone has witnessed the events that are the focus of the intervention. The group can react defensively or ignore the intervention, but it has been confronted and at least its consciousness of the events has been heightened.

I emphasize the confrontive nature of such interventions, even if they are mildly stated questions, because if they are based on observed events they draw attention irrevocably to something that has happened. It is for this reason that the process consultant should take care about the timing and wording of such interventions. In diagnostic interventions the consultant can claim ignorance when he asks an embarrassing question. But a question about some shared events in a meeting has much more potency because the group knows that the consultant has witnessed the events.

Agenda-managing interventions are only mildly confrontive, however, because they only draw attention to certain events and minimize a sharing of the observations and evaluations of the consultant. Such "feedback" from the consultant is addressed in the next chapter.

14

Confronting Through the Use of Feedback

Feedback of Observations or Other Data to Groups

There are basically two types of circumstances that call for this type of intervention. Case 1 is the situation where some group has agreed to a meeting in which interpersonal processes would be discussed, and has further agreed to have the consultant survey the members of the group for their individual reactions and feelings. The feedback of the survey results then serves as the opening agenda for the meeting. Case 2 is the situation where a group has already learned to discuss interpersonal process and has developed a need to supplement such discussion with more personal kinds of feedback. The meeting described in the previous section in which Apex executives gave each other feedback with the help of the consultant is a good example of the latter type of situation.

In both types of situation, there must be some readiness for feedback and some consensus that feedback of observations or interview results would be a legitimate activity for the group to undertake. There is nothing more tempting for the process consultant than to leap in with his own observations as soon as he has picked up some data on an interesting issue. If the consultant is to maintain congruence with the PC model, however, he must resist the temptation lest he put the group immediately on the defensive or undermine his own position by reporting something that does not make sense or is unpalatable to group members. The issue is not whether the observation is valid. The issue is whether the group is able and ready to understand and learn from the observation. Such ability and readiness must be built up before feedback can be useful.

The first type of intervention — reporting back data gathered from individuals — is a useful way to orient the group as to what its process issues may be. The previously cited case of the Fairview Company illustrates the use of this device as a way to open a discussion. By having group members write to me about the major organizational issues that they perceived, I was able to construct an agenda that would maximize the probability that the group would confront issues of importance to the members. At the first meeting of the group I presented the major categories of issues that the letters had revealed and tried to illustrate each issue by paraphrasing from one or more letters. The group was thus getting feedback, but the identity of the individual information source was protected.

I noticed during the three days of discussion that as the members became more comfortable with each other, they were increasingly able to make their own points and identify themselves openly with the various issues; they leaned less and less on me as the source of input. If the senior people in the group had reacted punitively to any of the issues brought up, the group would no doubt have avoided talking about those issues and there would have been less revelation of personal feelings. Fortunately the senior people were receptive, willing to listen to the issues, and able to work on them constructively.

In one of the divisions of the Apex Manufacturing Company, I followed a different procedure. After getting to know the top-management group through several group meetings, I suggested that it might be useful to interview and give feedback to the next level below the vice president. There was some concern on the part of the senior group that there might be a morale problem at this level. Initially I was asked merely to do an interview survey and report back to the top group. I declined this approach for reasons already mentioned: gathering data to report to a higher group would violate PC assumptions because it would not involve the sources of the data in analyzing their own process. I suggested instead that I conduct the interview with the ground rule that all my conclusions would first be reported back to the interviewee group, and that I would tell top management only those items that the group felt should be reported.[1]

The group would first have to sort the items and decide which things they could handle by themselves and which should be reported up the line of authority because they were under higher management control. The real value of the feedback should accrue to the group that initially provided the data; they should become involved in examining the issues they had brought up, and consider what they themselves might do about them.

The above-mentioned procedure was agreed upon by the top management. One vice president sent a memorandum to all members who would be involved in the interview program, informing them of the procedure, his commitment to it, and his hope that they would participate. I then followed up with individual appointments with each person concerned. At this initial appointment I recounted the origin of the idea, assured the interviewee that his *individual* responses would be entirely confidential, told him that I would summarize the data by department, and told him that he would see the group report and discuss it before any feedback went to his boss or higher management.

In the interview I asked each person to describe his job, tell what he found to be the major pluses and minuses in the job, describe what relationships he had to other groups, and explain how he felt about a series of specific job factors such as challenge, autonomy, supervision, facilities, salary and benefits, and so on. I later summarized the interviews in a report in which I tried to highlight what I saw to be common problem areas.

---

[1]This procedure was first brought to my attention as a method by Mr. Richard Beckhard.

All the respondents were then invited to a group meeting at which I passed out the summaries and explained that the purpose of the meeting was to examine the data, deleting or elaborating where necessary, and to determine which problem areas might be worked on by the group itself. We then went over the summary item by item, permitting as much discussion as any given item warranted.

The group meeting had its greatest utility in exposing the interviewees, in a systematic way, to interpersonal and group issues. For many of them, what they had thought to be private gripes turned out to be organizational problems that they could do something about. The attitude "Let top management solve all our problems" tended to be replaced with a viewpoint that differentiated between intragroup problems, intergroup problems, and those which were higher management's responsibility.

The interviewees not only gained more insight into organizational psychology but also responded positively to being involved in the process of data gathering itself. It symbolized to them top management's interest in them and concern for solving organizational problems. Reactions such as these are typical of other groups with whom I have tried the same approach.

Following the group meeting, the revised summary was then given to top management, in some cases individually, in others in a group. My own preference is to give it first individually, to provide for maximum opportunity to explain all the points, and then to follow up with a group discussion of the implications of the data revealed in the interviews. Where the direct supervisor of the group is involved, I have often supplemented the group report with an individual report, which extracts all the comments made by interviewees concerning the strengths and weaknesses of the supervisor's style of management. These focused feedback items have usually proved of great value to the manager, but they should be provided only if the manager initially asked for this type of feedback.

In giving either individual or group feedback from the interview summary, my role is to ensure understanding of the data and to stimulate acceptance of it so that remedial action of some sort can be effectively undertaken. Once the expectation has been built that top management will do something, there is great risk of lowering morale if the report is merely read, without being acted upon in some manner. Incidentally, it is the process consultant's job to ensure that top management *makes this commitment initially* and that high-level officials understand that when the interviews are completed there will be some demands for action. If management merely wants information without willingness to do something about the information, the consultant should not do the interviews in the first place. The danger is too great that management will not like what it hears and will suppress the whole effort; such a course will only lead to a deterioration of morale.

The results of interviews (or questionnaires) do not necessarily have to go beyond the group that is interested in them. One of the simplest and most helpful things a group can do to enhance its own functioning is to have the consultant interview the members individually and report back to the *group as a whole* a summary of its own members' feelings. It is a way of hauling crucial data out into the open without the risk of personal exposure of any individual if he feels the data collected about him are damaging or that the analysis of such data will result in conclusions that are overcritical of his performance.

Feedback to Individuals

A more detailed analysis of how to give feedback can be found in Chapter 8, "Appraising Performance and Giving Feedback," but some comments should be made in this context about the circumstances of when and how the process consultant can and should get involved in feedback to clients. Feedback from the consultant to an individual is an appropriate intervention when (1) some data have been gathered about the individual (by either interview or direct observation), and (2) the individual has indicated a readiness to hear such feedback.

In the case where a number of subordinates have been interviewed, some of the comments they make will deal with their reactions to the boss's behavior. If the superior has agreed beforehand to listen to the others' reactions, it is quite appropriate for the consultant to describe the range of comments to him and to assist in interpreting the comments. If the consultant feels that the manager is interested and shows a readiness to listen and learn, it is entirely appropriate for the consultant to share these observations.

In order for feedback to be effective, the consultant must be able to ask the right questions, observe the relevant behavioral events, and give the feedback in a manner that will facilitate learning on the part of the recipient. The behavior asked about or observed must be relevant to the task performance of the group and to the goals of the total consultation project. The manner in which the feedback is given must reflect sensitivity to the blind spots or areas of defensiveness of the recipient. Feedback must be concrete, descriptive, verifiable, timely, and specific.

The consultant must be prepared for defensiveness or too facile verbal acceptance, both of which imply a denial of the feedback. He must know how to impart potentially threatening information without demeaning the recipient. As I think back over my various consulting experiences, unquestionably the ones with the most disastrous results were those where I fed back "facts" without any concern for the feelings of the recipient. The facts were then denied, and I was politely but firmly invited to terminate the relationship.

The giving of individual feedback can be illustrated from several cases. In the Apex Manufacturing Company I met with each of the vice presidents whose groups had been interviewed and gave them a list of comments that had been made about their respective managerial styles. I knew each man well and felt that he would be able to accept the kinds of comments that were made. In each case we scheduled at least a one-hour session so we could talk in detail about any items that were unclear and/or threatening.

These discussions usually become counseling sessions to help the individual overcome some of the negative effects that were implied in the feedback data. Since I knew that I would be having sessions such as these, I urged each interviewee to talk at length about the style of his boss and what he did or did not like about it. In cases where the boss was an effective manager, I found a tendency for subordinates to make only a few vague generalizations that I knew would be useless as feedback. By probing for specific incidents or descriptions, it was possible to identify just what the boss did that subordinates liked or did not like.

In the Delta Manufacturing Company I was invited by the division manager to observe and comment on the regular staff meetings. In addition I held discussions periodically with the manager and was invited to comment on any aspects of his behavior that I had observed. He had formulated fairly specific goals for his meeting and was interested in the degree to which he was meeting those goals in his role as chairman. He asked for feedback from group members at the end of meetings but also sought my observations.

In the workshops run for the Central Chemical Company, I concentrated primarily on the co-trainer, the member of the company who was working with me but wanted to learn how to run workshops like these on his own. After each session I would give him feedback on his participation in it and, incidentally, solicit his feedback on my participation. As we learned to reciprocate with our observations, the feedback process became more meaningful to both of us.

As a rule I do not hesitate to ask members of the client organization to give me feedback on my own behavior as a consultant. Although they are usually reluctant to do so early in the relationship, I find that as we get to know each other they become comfortable in telling me where I was effective or ineffective with them or with others. The ability to give me feedback in the two-person setting is, of course, an important skill that should transfer as an ability to be more open and direct with others in authority positions. The ability to give me feedback is also an important indicator of how well the problem of dependence on the consultant has been solved.

Summary

A major category of confrontive interventions that are designed to influence process are the various kinds of feedback that the process consultant gives to individuals or groups, or that they give to each other with the aid of processes designed in part by the consultant. The most important issue in deciding whether and when to engage in such feedback processes is how ready the group or individual is to deal with feedback, and how much the client has been involved in the decision to get some feedback. It rarely works out for the process consultant to decide unilaterally to give feedback, even though he may have observed events that are dramatic in their learning potential.

15

Coaching, Counseling, and Structural Suggestions

The last two categories of confrontive intervention are coaching/counseling and structural suggestions. As was stated before, I find these to be relatively rare compared to the other categories discussed, and they are in principle more powerful. It is therefore all the more important either that the client have a voice in when these types of interventions are made, or that the consultant take great care to ensure that the client is ready for them if he makes them unilaterally.

Coaching or Counseling

The giving of feedback to individuals or to groups almost invariably leads to coaching or counseling sessions. The manger may learn that he somehow fails to hear certain members of the group, that he does not give enough recognition for good performance, or that he is too unapproachable when the subordinate needs help. Inevitably his next question is "How can I change my behavior to achieve better results?" Similarly, a group may learn that its members see the meetings as dull or unfruitful; inevitably the members then ask, "How can we make our meetings more interesting and productive?"

There are two cautions that the consultant must keep uppermost in his mind before answering the above questions:

1. Don't respond until you are sure that the group (or individual) has really understood the feedback and has been able to relate it to concrete observable behavior.
2. Don't respond until you are sure that the group member (or manager) has begun an active process of trying to solve the problem for himself.

If the consultant is not sure on point 1, he should continue to ask such questions as "What does that comment mean to you in terms of how you see yourself?" "Can you think of anything you do that might give people that impression?" Or "What do you think the giver of the comment was trying to get across to you?"

If the consultant is not sure on point 2, he can ask such questions as "Do you see anything in your own behavior that you could change?" "What might you do differently to create a different reaction?" Or "Do you really want to change your behavior?"

If the consultant receives a response like "I'm paying *you* to give me advice," he must reassess the state of the relationship and the readiness of the recipient of the feedback to work on the problem area. If the feedback has been sincerely sought and has been understood, most likely the recipient will have ideas and share these with the consultant. The consultant's role then becomes one of adding alternatives to those already brought up by the client and helping the client to analyze the costs and benefits of the various alternatives that have been mentioned.

I do not wish in this short volume to go into the theory and practice of counseling, but I do wish to underline the basic congruence between theories of counseling and the theory of process consultation that I am presenting here. In both cases it is essential to help the client improve his ability to observe and process data about himself, to help him accept and learn from feedback, and to help him become an active participant with the counselor/consultant in identifying and solving his own problems.

In all of the companies with which I have worked, there have arisen multiple opportunities to coach and counsel individuals or groups. There does not seem to be any particular pattern of timing to such sessions. Rather, I have had to be ready to sit down with people when *they* were ready to examine some of their own behavior and consider alternatives.

The major difference between being only a counselor and being a process consultant has been the fact that my data gathering has given me information and perspectives that a counselor often does not have. I have usually observed my client in action and heard what other people have said about him. This additional knowledge, when fed into the counseling sessions, enriches the choice of alternatives that can be considered and opens up many of the problem areas to more concrete discussion.

For example, I have spent some hours with a manager who sees himself as a very progressive force in a rather conservative organization. My observations, and what others say about him, would suggest that he himself is rather conservative in his behavior. His *ideas* are progressive, but his actual behavior tends to be stultifying to others. Our individual sessions are most productive when we can examine his self-image against what others say and what I have observed. As this manager learned to view his conservatism in action, he realized that he undermines some of his own progressive ideas. This realization has led to some marked changes of behavior and an increase in his effectiveness.

There is a close similarity between interventions that draw the group's attention to certain kinds of process issues and what I choose to call counseling (or coaching) types of interventions. One of the most common opportunities to coach or counsel is to intervene when a particular event has occurred that is typical of some problem the group is trying to overcome. At these times the consultant can be most effective by pointing out what has just occurred and inviting the group to examine the consequences. He is giving feedback at a timely moment in order to help the group to become more effective.

Case Examples

The first case illustrates both the issue of feedback and how that leads to counseling. In one company's executive committee meetings I noticed that the group seemed to have low confidence in one of its members, the marketing manager. This lack of confidence was evident in the degree to which others ignored him, argued with him, and denigrated him outside the meetings. Every time this man attempted to explain any of his actions, decisions, or plans in the meetings, one of the more aggressive members would interrupt him and either answer for him or elaborate on what he thought the marketing manager had said.

The group seemed to expect this person to be weak and passive, and confirmed their expectation by preventing him from being anything else. I decided to intervene at the point where the behavior was most visible (just after the marketing manager had been ignored or interrupted on some issue) and tell the group that I observed the pattern repeatedly (confrontive feedback).

The group then expressed some interest in hearing whether the marketing manager did indeed feel cut off. He expressed some rather strong feelings confirming my observations. Once these feelings were known to the other members, they began to listen more attentively to him. As they did so, they discovered that he had a lot to contribute and was anything but "weak" and "fuzzy-headed," as they had believed. Group members then began to trust his decisions more and became more comfortable in delegating authority to him.

After each meeting both the chairman of the group and the marketing manager asked to see me privately. The chairman wanted me to advise him on how he could run the meeting better so that this kind of thing would not happen again, and to give him feedback after each meeting on how he was doing as a chairman.

The marketing manager asked me how he could learn to be more assertive and not collude with the aggressive members by allowing himself to be shut down. In both cases I set up a series of meetings right after the formal meeting to counsel each of these managers (note that the agenda for the counseling was their own).

In another group, the difficulty was initially related to the manner in which the boss of the group interacted with the members. The boss wanted the group members to be strong, self-reliant, confident decision makers. He said this explicitly and his behavior implied it. I observed on repeated occasions that if any group member showed weakness in any form (not knowing what he wanted, having unclear plans, being unable to answer a critical question from another member), the head of the group would become angry and belabor the person for many minutes on end. The more the head of the group pressed, the more silent, embarrassed, and unsure the target person became.

In talking to such persons later, I often found that the only feeling they sensed in the head of the group was blind anger, and this made them so defensive that they could not hear what he really wanted of them. In each such conversation I found myself counseling the individual member to try to listen for the feelings other than anger. For example, I wondered whether the boss was anxious that things were out of control and that this showed up as anger. I urged members to try to reassure the boss rather than to defend themselves.

On several occasions I tried to interrupt the process in midstream and collect feelings both from the person being belabored and from other members of the group (agenda managing and controlling). In addition I gave direct feedback to the group head, both in front of the group and later privately, concerning the impact his behavior was having *on me*. I expressed puzzlement and asked the boss what he was actually feeling, and advised him to try to be more accurate in communicating what he really felt.

This led to some self-analysis on his part and the request to have me counsel him between meetings. His behavior in the group gradually shifted away from communication of anger toward communication of anxiety and disappointment, which in turn made it possible for the group to home in on the issue that was really bothering them.

Finally, I had occasion to attend one of the group meetings when the boss was absent. The group used the opportunity to inquire what I thought they should do in managing their boss's feelings better, and I found myself in a counseling role to the entire group. We then spent over an hour analyzing what was going on, examining options, and deciding how to behave differently in the future, with my role being primarily that of a coach.

Structural Suggestions

As I indicated at the outset of this chapter, this kind of intervention is rare, largely because it violates some of the basic assumptions of the PC model. The consultant is rarely in a position to suggest how work should be allocated, or how communication patterns should be altered, or how committees should be organized. The most he can do is help the manager to assess the consequences of different alternatives or suggest alternatives that have not been considered.

For example, when the Apex Manufacturing Company went from a functional to a product-line organization, I noticed that communication among the functional people (for example, in marketing and engineering) decreased markedly. During group meetings there were complaints and some recriminations about the possible error of having reorganized.

My intervention was designed to draw attention to the fact that *any* form of organization has both strengths and weaknesses. Hence the manager needs to make an effort to create informal structures to compensate for the weaknesses created by the formal structure. I embodied this point in a short memo (see Appendix B) and asked for time on the agenda to discuss the point.

The company eventually adopted a committee structure that brought the functional specialists together on a regular basis and thus reduced the communication gap that had resulted from the reorganization.

The consultant must make it quite clear that he does not propose any particular solution as the best one. However frustrating it might be to the client, the consultant must work to create a situation where the client's ability to generate his own solutions is enhanced. The consultant wants to increase problem-solving ability, not to solve any particular problem.

In my experience there has been only one class of exceptions to the above "rule." If the client wants to set up some meetings specifically for the purpose of working on organizational or interpersonal problems, or wants to design a data-gathering method, then the consultant indeed does have some relevant expertise that he should bring to bear. From his own experience he knows better than the client the pros and cons of interviews or questionnaires; he knows better what questions to ask, how to organize the data, and how to organize feedback meetings; he knows better the right sequence of events leading up to a good discussion of interpersonal process in a committee. In such matters, therefore, I am quite direct and positive in suggesting procedures, who should be involved in them, who should be told what, and how the whole project should be handled.

For example, recall that in the Apex Manufacturing Company the president decided at one of their all-day meetings to try to give feedback to all the members. He asked me to suggest a procedure for doing this. In this instance I was not at all reluctant to suggest, with as much force and logic as I could command, a particular procedure that I thought would work well. Similarly, when it was proposed to interview all the members of a department, I suggested exactly how this procedure should be set up. I explained that all the members had to be briefed by the department manager, that a group feedback meeting would have to be held, and so on. I have not been at all hesitant to refuse to design a questionnaire study if I thought it was inappropriate, or to suggest canceling a meeting on interpersonal process if I thought the group was not ready.

In conclusion, the process consultant should not withhold his expertise on matters of the learning process itself; but he should be very careful not to confuse being an expert on *how to help an organization to learn* with being an expert on the *actual management problems* that the organization is trying to solve. The same logic applies to the evaluation of individuals: I will under no circumstances evaluate an individual's ability to manage or solve work-related problems; but I will evaluate an individual's readiness to participate in an interview survey of his group or a feedback meeting. If I feel that his presence might undermine some other goals that the organization is trying to accomplish, I will seek to find a solution that will bypass this individual. These are often difficult judgments to make, but the process consultant cannot evade them if he defines the *overall health of the organization* as his basic target. However, he must always attempt to be fair to both the individual and the organization. If no course of action can be found without hurting either, then the whole project should probably be postponed.

I can give two further examples of structural interventions. In Company G, not previously referred to, I have worked for some time with a member of the corporate management-development group. I have functioned primarily as an adviser, counselor, and sounding board on various programs being developed by the group. The organization does not have major aspirations in the organizational development direction, although there is a growing interest in this kind of activity. Sometime last year, the inside manager was requested to consider a training program for all of the key marketing people in the various divisions of the company.

I was called in to help design this program and to function as a staff member in it. My responsibilities included the recruiting of another staff member, helping members of management formulate their hopes and needs for the program, and then helping to design the actual program. This required a shift in my role from process consultant to an expert resource on the design and execution of a management-training program.

In my relationship with Company G, I find myself making this switch from time to time. The role switching works because I have worked with this client company for a number of years and the client contact is himself comfortable in playing and adapting to different roles in the relationship. The primary contact also functions as a point of communication with other groups in the organization where process consultation is needed from time to time. For example, I have worked with a sales group in one of the divisions of the company on an interview-feedback project, in determining how the members of the operating sales force in one region were viewing their job and in helping management to reassess the overall style of operation in the sales function.

The second example comes from the Boyd Consumer Goods Company. My primary work in this organization was to meet with the top-management group and to counsel individual members of the group. Last year I was asked by the personnel director to become involved in the annual manpower survey and to help the organization design a more coherent overall approach to management development. To accomplish this task I asked to be a part of the manpower committee. During the meetings I attempted to assess the needs of the organization and the kind of program that would meet these needs. In doing this I was beginning to shift toward being an expert resource and abandoning the process consultant role.

It seemed to me, as I listened to the discussions, that the group would fall short of generating a clear concept of a program in the time it had allotted for itself; hence I intervened structurally and suggested a multicomponent program of self-development, systematic use of internal and external training, and a revision of policies of recruiting and utilizing people in the organization. All of the points were extrapolations of what members of the committee wanted to do, but I put them together into a total framework and made some effort to "sell" it to the group. The group adopted the program and made a proposal of it to other members of management and the board.

In looking back on this intervention, I have wondered whether the structural nature of it was indeed warranted and whether my own goals were truly accomplished. There is some evidence that the program has been bought in principle and that everyone agrees to it intellectually, but there has been relatively little move to implement it. At least one possibility as to why it has not been more systematically implemented is that I went too far beyond the group with my intervention — somehow the group lost ownership of the program and hence felt no real commitment to implement it. If this hypothesis is correct, it illustrates nicely the fine line between process and expert consultation and the inherent dangers of structural interventions.

Summary

In the past several chapters I have tried to draw attention to the varieties of intervention that the process consultant uses.

I hope it is clear to the reader that the essence of the PC model is to continuously rediagnose and to act accordingly. Therefore, one cannot specify particular recipes for intervention or particular sequences that should be used in any given project. A sequence that may work in Company A may be all wrong in Company B. Instead, the consultant must be ready to intervene in a variety of ways as opportunities arise and as his judgment tells him certain actions are appropriate. He must be flexible enough to take advantage of opportunities based on his own judgments.

The following are kinds of intervention that were reviewed:

1. Agenda managing through questions, through process-analysis periods, through meetings devoted to interpersonal and group process, and through theory inputs on various process issues.
2. Various kinds of feedback sessions to individuals or groups, based either on observed data or on data obtained in interviews.
3. Coaching or counseling, which occurs either in specific sessions devoted to that purpose or as part of an ongoing interaction in a group.
4. Structural suggestions pertaining to process-oriented meetings or other parts of the consultation project.

A more refined analysis of intervention types can be found in volume 2 of *Process Consultation* (1987).

16

Evaluation of Results and Disengagement

So far in this book we have examined in some detail the thinking and activities of a process consultant. We have not concentrated on the big picture: what kinds of outcome or result does the process consultant look for over a period of time, how does he measure these outcomes, and how does he decide at some point to reduce his involvement with the client system?

These questions are not easy to answer because the goals of PC cannot be stated in simple measurable terms. The ultimate goal of any organization-development effort is, of course, improved organizational performance. Organization-development efforts as I have defined them always involve activities that are carried out with the philosophy and attitudes of PC and, therefore, one would expect to achieve effectiveness by changing some of the *values* of the organization and by increasing the *task and interpersonal process skills* of key managers. Performance is, in turn, related to these value changes and increases of skill. In the short run, then, the consultant looks for evidence that certain values are changing and that certain skills are increasing.

Values to Be Changed
Through Process Consultation

Task Versus Interpersonal Concern

The single most important value to be changed in any OD effort concerns the relative attention given to task versus human concerns. Most managers start with the value that the most important concerns of management are efficient task performance primarily, and human relations secondarily (or as time permits). The problem for the process consultant is to change this value — make the manager feel that human relations and the management of interpersonal and group events are at least as important as immediate task performance.

The logic behind this value is that for the manager his task can be accomplished only through other people; hence effective interpersonal relations become a prime means to the end of efficient task performance. Organizations in the end are nothing more than networks of human relationships. If these networks do not function effectively, there is nothing with which to perform the tasks to be accomplished.

Content Versus Process Focus

A second value that has to be changed in any OD effort concerns the relative attention given to the content of the work and the structure of the organization versus the process by which work is done and the structure of that process. Managers tend to focus much more on the content of decisions, interactions, and communications. They tend to devalue the importance of "personality," of "feelings," and of "how things are done," or they attempt to dodge such process-related issues by perpetual redesign of the formal structure of the organization.

The process consultant faces the problem of showing managers that processes in the organization follow patterns that can be studied and understood, and that have important consequences for organizational performance. Most important, processes can be rationally changed and adapted to increase the effectiveness of performance. Therefore, one should attempt to improve the organization through a joint consideration of the content and formal structure, on the one hand, and of the processes of the organization, on the other hand.

Short-run Output Versus Long-range Effectiveness

A third value concerns the relative attention given to short-run output versus long-range effectiveness. Most managers feel that every hour of every day should be occupied with activities that have an immediate output. The process consultant knows from his experience that the diagnosis of process events often involves periods of slow and calm analysis that may at first appear to be a terrible waste of time. He must change the manager's value system so that he becomes tolerant of such periods, realizing that the time invested in building effective task processes and interpersonal relations leads to much quicker and more effective ultimate task performance.

Instant Solutions Versus Perpetual Rediagnosis

A fourth value that the process consultant must inculcate is the acceptance of the need for perpetual diagnosis as an alternative to insistence on instant solutions or generalizations and principles by which to operate. I assume that the rate of change in the environment (and, therefore, within organizations) will increase, and that this in turn will require an increase in the organization's ability to diagnose both the environment and itself. A principle that holds up for the next six months may be invalid within a year.

The manager must accept perpetual diagnosis of process as a way of life if he is to avoid obsolescence and organizational failure. Ideally, the manager would not merely accept this value grudgingly but would discover that perpetual diagnosis can be fun and lead to perpetually better day-to-day task performance. I am not advocating what so many managers seem to fear — that if they do too much diagnosis they will be unable to be decisive when an occasion demands it. I am advocating that decisions be made, within the time constraints imposed by the task requirements, but that they be made in terms of a *diagnosis*, however short, rather than a policy or general principle that may no longer have any validity.

In summary, the process consultant attempts to change the manager's attitudes and values in the direction of more concern for human problems, process issues, long-run effectiveness, and the diagnostic process itself as a way of achieving organizational adaptability. By implication, one major way to assess the results of a PC effort is to gauge the degree to which these values have taken hold in key managers. Such an assessment cannot be made formally or through some kind of specific measuring tool. It must be made by the consultant through observation of the activities of managers in the organization, or by the managers themselves.

Skills to Be Learned

As I have been repeating throughout this volume, the most important skill to be imparted to the client is the *ability to diagnose and work on his own problems in the task, interpersonal, group, and organizational area.* Initially the process consultant has more knowledge and skill than the client. As the PC effort progresses, he should be able to observe an increase in the knowlege and skill of the various managers who have been involved.

One of the best indicators of the growth of such skills is the willingness of various groups or teams to tackle process-analysis periods or agenda-review periods by themselves. How willing are they to assign an observer role, and how skillful are they in picking out key group events, in sharing feelings, in reviewing group action?

It should be clear that a willingness to engage in activities that initially have been the consultant's reflects a change in values. Even if a given manager were able to engage in more self-diagnostic processes, he might resist such an activity if none of the values cited above had changed. On the other hand, willingness reflecting a value change is not enough if there has not been a corresponding development of skill.

The assessment of the skill of the client system in diagnosing and working on its own problems must, as in the case of values, be made by observations on the part of the consultant and/ or by the client system itself. It is important that managers feel confident in solving their own problems, and solving them effectively. Even if the consultant doubts that the level of skill reached is sufficient, he must be prepared to back off if members of the client system themselves feel they are able to go ahead without his help.

Case Examples

In the Apex Manufacturing Company, considerable value change and skill growth occurred over the course of the first year. During this period I spent a great deal of time in two major activities: (1) sitting in on various meetings of the top-management group, and (2) conducting interview and feedback surveys of various key groups, as managers decided they wanted such interviews done. In addition there were periods of individual counseling, usually resulting from data revealed in the interviews.

I have already given examples of the kinds of specific activities that occurred in the group meetings, interviews, and feedback sessions. It was clear that with increasing experience, the group was learning to tune in to its own internal processes (skill), was beginning to pay more attention to these and to give over more meeting time to analysis of interpersonal feelings and events (value change), and was able to manage its own agenda and do its diagnosis without my presence (skill).

The group first discovered this from having to conduct some of its all-day meetings in my absence. Where such meetings used to be devoted entirely to work content, the group found that even in my absence they could discuss task and interpersonal process with profit. The members themselves described this change as one of "climate." The group felt more open and effective; members felt they could trust each other more; information was flowing more freely; less time was being wasted on oblique communications or political infighting.

During the second year, my involvement was considerably reduced, although I worked on some specific projects. The company had set up a committee to develop a management-development program. I was asked to sit in with this committee and help in the development of a program. After a number of meetings, it became clear to me that the kind of program the group needed was one in which the content was not too heavily predetermined. The problems of different managers were sufficiently different to require that a formula be found for discussing the whole range of problems.

One of the reflections of the value change that had taken place in the managers was their recognition that they should be prime participants in any program they might invent. If a program was not exciting or beneficial enough to warrant the committee's time, it could hardly be imposed on the rest of the organization.

We developed a model that involved a series of small-group meetings at each of which the group would set its own agenda. After every third meeting or so, a larger management group would be convened for a lecture and discussion period on some highly relevant topic. Once the first group (the committee plus others at the vice president level) had completed six to eight meetings, each member of the original group would become the chairman for a group at the next lower level of the organization. These ten or so next-level groups would then meet for six to eight sessions around agenda items developed by themselves. In the meantime the lecture series would continue. After each series of meetings at a given organizational level, the model would be reassessed and either changed or continued at the next lower level with the previous members again becoming group chairmen.

My role in this whole enterprise was, first, to help the group to invent the idea; second, to meet with the original group as a facilitator of the group's efforts to become productive; third, to serve as a resource on topics to be covered and lecturers to be used in the lecture series; and fourth, to appear as an occasional lecturer in the lecture series or as a source of input at a small-group meeting. As this procedure took form, my involvement was gradually reduced, although I still meet with the original committee to review the overall concept.

In subsequent months I met occasionally with individual members of the original group and with the group as a whole. My function during these meetings was to be a sounding board, to contribute points of view that might not have been represented among the members, and to help the group assess its own level of functioning. I was able to provide the group with some perspective on its own growth as a group because I could more easily see changes in values and skills.

It has also been possible for the group to enlist my help with specific interpersonal problems. A measure of the growth of the group has been its ability to decide when and how to use my help, and to make those decisions validly from my point of view in terms of where I felt I could constructively help. This relationship of being called in from time to time as new issues arose continued for many years, and I considered my work with this organization to have been generally successful in terms of getting values and skills across.

In the Boyd Consumer Goods Company, my participation was initially similar, but for a variety of reasons changes in the organization occurred much more slowly. The top-management group accepted many of the values at an intellectual level but has not really committed itself to trying to make them work. Some members of the group have worked much harder at this than others. At the level of skill development, the group has experimented with a variety of techniques, such as having a member of the group be an observer and then report back. These activities have had a noticeable (although not a great) impact.

Part of the problem in this company is that they have had to fight a number of traditions that are, in varying degrees, out of line with the kinds of values I espoused. They have also faced a number of crises that required immediate action and that eroded efforts to concentrate on increasing diagnostic and interpersonal skills. This case illustrates that if the basic culture of the organization involves assumptions that are out of line with the values underlying PC, it is difficult to achieve clear-cut changes. For the culture itself to change, a more intensive organization change program would have had to be launched (Schein, 1985).

Over a period of months I continued to meet both with individuals and with the group as a whole. My activities involved counseling members of the group and keeping a gentle but firm pressure on members of the system to become more open, trusting, and, thereby, effective. Recently the group decided on its own to hold a two-day meeting at which some strong personal feelings were shared by members of the group. Although the experience was traumatic for one or two members, the feeling of most was that it had been constructive and they looked forward to more of the same at some later time. My role in the meantime was to help them to understand the emotional experience they had been through and show them how to turn it into a constructive experience. After some months our contact was reduced, and I have since lost touch with what is going on. In looking back on this experience, I feel that not much was accomplished, given the amount of effort, but the group could move only as fast as its culture would allow.

In the Central Chemical Company, I worked in a more discrete fashion around projects that were scheduled well in advance and that were evaluated right after each workshop by the inside consultant and me. The initial workshops were done within a single division, and the decision whether to continue depended on whether other divisions would decide to hold some kind of planned change activity. Two other divisions decided to go ahead, so I became involved in planning, executing, and evaluating these particular programs while periodically visiting with the corporate inside consultants on overall strategy.

When the workshops were over some several years later the emphasis in the overall effort shifted to more use of inside consultants, so my work was terminated. The overall effort was considered to be highly successful in that it got a process started that could then be taken over by internal resources, but a great deal of change had been accomplished already by the externally influenced workshops.

In the Delta Manufacturing Company, I found the key group to be from the start relatively high in its acceptance of OD values and in its level of skill. After a dozen or so meetings the group and I reviewed the project and decided that for the moment nothing more was needed.

As problems developed, the group would resume contact with me. Some months later the group had to be expanded because the whole division that was involved was to be expanded. With the expansion came some potential new problems. Because the diagnostic skill of the group was already high, I was called in again to make some plans for a longer meeting at which some of the new problems would be explored in depth.

I continued to work sporadically with this organization for a number of years, always with a sense of effectiveness because they had learned when and how to use external help.

Conclusion

Process consultation is an emergent process. To put simple boundaries on it would be difficult. Similarly, it is difficult to give overall evaluations. One can look at gradual changes that occur in the culture of the client organization; one can look at the results of specific projects, such as an interview-feedback cycle; and one can assess the immediate impact of an intervention in a group. But one cannot measure specific indicators, however, much this might be desirable. In the end, the outcome of a period of PC must be judged jointly by members of the client system and the consultant. Both must make a judgment of whether to continue the relationship and in what manner to continue it.

If, in the judgment of either party, there should be a reduction of involvement, how is this process accomplished?

Disengagement: Reducing Involvement with the Client System

The process of disengagement has, in most of my experiences, been characterized by the following features:

1. Reduced involvement is a mutually agreed upon decision rather than a unilateral decision by consultant or client.
2. Involvement does not generally drop to zero but may continue at a very low level.
3. The door is always open from my point of view for further work with the client if the client desires it.

I would like to comment on each of these points, and give some examples.

1. Joint Decisions

In most of my consulting relationships there has come a time when either I felt that nothing more could be accomplished and/or some members of the client system felt the need to continue on their own. To facilitate a reduction of involvement, I usually check at intervals of several months to see whether the client feels that the pattern should remain as is or should be altered.

In some cases where I have felt that a sufficient amount had been accomplished, I have found that the client did not feel the same way and wanted the relationship to continue on a one-day-per-week basis. In other cases I have been confronted by the client, as in the Apex Manufacturing Company, with the statement that my continued attendance in the operational group meetings was no longer desirable from their point of view. As the president put it, I was beginning to sound too much like a regular member to be of much use. I concurred in the decision and reduced my involvement to periodic all-day meetings of the group, although the initiative for inviting me remained entirely with the group. Had I not concurred, we would have negotiated until a mutually satisfactory arrangement had been agreed on.

I have sometimes been in the situation of arguing that I remain fully involved even when the client wanted to reduce involvement, and in many cases I was able to obtain the client's concurrence. I have also been involved frequently in arguing for a reduction of involvement either because I felt that nothing more could be accomplished or that the client was becoming too dependent on me.

The negotiation that surrounds a reduction of involvement is, in fact, a good opportunity for the consultant to diagnose the state of the client system. The kinds of arguments that are brought up in support of continuing (or terminating) provide a solid basis for determining how much value and skill change has occurred.

The reader may feel that since the client is paying for services, he certainly has the right to make unilateral decisions about whether to continue the services. My point is that if the consultation process has even partially achieved its goals, there should develop sufficient trust between consultant and client to enable both to make the decision on rational grounds. Here again, it is important that the consultant not be economically dependent on any one client, or his own diagnostic ability may become biased by his need to continue to earn fees.

2. Involvement Not Zero

If the client and consultant agree on a reduced involvement, both should recognize that this does not necessarily mean a complete termination. In fact, a complete termination is not desirable because the diagnosis on which reduced involvement is based may not be accurate enough to warrant termination. A more desirable arrangement is to drop the level to perhaps a half day every three or four weeks, or attendance only at certain kinds of special meetings, or an interview with key members of the client system once every two or three months. Through this mechanism the client and the consultant can reassess periodically how things are going.

In the Boyd Consumer Goods Company, there was a period where I felt that a plateau had been reached. At this point I suggested that I reduce my involvement to a half day every other week, and even then only if specific individuals wanted to have some time to talk over problems with me. After a few months at this reduced level, a number of events made it more important than ever for the top-management group to increase their level of effectiveness. The group decided to have more meetings and asked me to become reinvolved at an increased level. This decision was much easier to negotiate from a reduced involvement than it would have been from a situation where I had terminated the relationship completely.

In my relationship with the Apex and Fairview companies, there were long periods where I did not pay any visits, but it was understood that as problems or issues came up the client was free to call on me with the expectation that I would respond positively. The only problem with this kind of arrangement is that it becomes difficult for the consultant to plan his time. Obviously, if several clients decide to increase their involvement all at the same time, it may be impossible for the consultant to respond. If this occurs, the consultant has to be open about his dilemma and determine from the various clients whether they can wait for a month or so. I have found from experience that I can carry about four clients at any given time, with two of them being more active (one half day every week), while two others are dormant (an occasional visit every three weeks to a month).

3. Reinvolvement Is Always Possible

This point is closely related to the previous one, but I want to separate it to bring out a special aspect of the obligation of the process consultant. In any process consulting relationship with a client, I think the consultant should make it clear that the door is always open to further work once the relationship has begun. The reason for this obligation is that a good relationship with a consultant is difficult for a client to develop. Once both the consultant and the client have invested effort in building such a relationship, it does not terminate psychologically even if there are prolonged periods of no contact. I have had the experience with a number of clients of not seeing them for many months and yet being able to tune in on the group very quickly once contact has been reestablished.

As a general rule it should be the client who reestablishes contact, but I would not advocate sticking to this rigidly. I have, after some period of no contact, called a client and asked if I could talk with him to find out what was going on. In several cases such a call was welcomed and served as the basis for some additional counseling or process observation. The consultant must be careful not to violate his role by selling himself back to the client. It must be an honest inquiry that can comfortably be turned down by the client should he desire to do so. I have been turned down often enough to know that there is nothing inherent in the situation to force an artificial contact. Rather, it sometimes helps a client who wanted help anyway to ask for it in a face-saving way.

Summary

I have spelled out several values and skills that the process consultant desires to pass on to the client system. The values are a more balanced concern for human issues along with task issues, process along with content, long-range effectiveness along with short-run efficiency, and perpetual diagnosis along with seeking rules, principles, and generalizations.

In the skill area it is primarily the ability to diagnose and work on task and interpersonal processes that is crucial, in that the ultimate goal of PC is for the client to be able to recognize and solve his own problems.

Evaluation of progress can be judged by both the consultant and the client, but since PC is an emergent unpredictable process, evaluation itself becomes a perpetual activity rather than a set activity or stage.

If either the consultant or the client feels that involvement should be reduced, a process of disengagement is desirable, but the reduced involvement should be jointly decided, should not be psychologically permanent, and should allow for either the consultant or the client to feel free to call for the consultant's reinvolvement.

17

Process Consultation
in Perspective

Why Process Consultation?

This book will, I hope, serve several purposes. First, I want to introduce a model of the consultation process that I believe describes what the typical consultant does (or should do) in an organization-development effort. Many of the volumes written on OD give an overview of the OD effort but do not give a detailed view of the consultant's day-to-day operation. This revised volume 1 with the more detailed and elaborated volume 2 should provide the kind of detail that is often missing.

Second, I want to explain as clearly as I can what has gone on between me as a consultant and a number of clients I have had over the years. I have found that some of my colleagues have entertained some remarkable misconceptions about what I do when I visit a company. I want to clear away some of these misconceptions.

Third, I want to contribute to the general theory of organizational consultation by illustrating clearly one style of working with an organization. In view of the increasing amount of research and consultation in complex organizations, it is important to know clearly what one is doing. I hope I have clarified some of the issues by laying out the concept of process consultation.

I should like to close this volume by making a few general comments about process consultation in relation to other kinds of activities, as a way of giving some perspective to this procedure. Process consultation, first of all, is *a way of studying organizations.* I believe very much in Lewin's dictum: "If you want to understand something, try to change it." Much of the consultant's satisfaction comes from the combination of exercising diagnostic and intervention skills while being constantly exposed to organizational process from which one learns what goes on in organizations. This exposure has enriched and sharpened my teaching and research skills and has led me to attempt to articulate this way of clinically studying an organization (Schein, 1987b).

As I mentioned in my original preface, one of my colleagues once asked me why I "wasted" time teaching managers elementary psychology when I could be doing research that would influence thousands. The first answer is that PC is anything but the teaching of elementary psychology. For me it is a complex process of producing changes in the organization that are not achievable by any amount of good writing. The change process is one not merely of transmitting ideas but of changing values and of teaching skills. I derive far more satisfaction from improving an organization's effectiveness than I would from teaching a few managers some psychology that they might not know how to apply anyway.

The second answer is that research done on organizations by people who do not get close to organizational processes has, to me, a kind of unreal quality about it — unreal because in focusing on concepts that are so far removed from the immediate experiences of members of the organization, one does not know how to generalize from the results. On the other hand, the kind of diagnosis that occurs when one conducts a series of interviews or observes groups in action brings organizational phenomena to life. For me consultation has been one important way to do research.

The third, and perhaps most important, answer is that my

teaching would be sterile without the kind of "feel" one gets from close contact with organizations. I could, of course, periodically immerse myself completely by taking a job in an organization. Apart from the fact that I would not like the dislocation involved, I am not sure that such a complete transition is necessary to get the kind of feel I am talking about.

Does Process Consultation Have Analogues?

The process consultant often operates in organizations in much the same way as a general practitioner does in medicine; he is, in a sense, an organizational internist and often an organizational psychiatrist. The analogy holds if one thinks of the consultant as helping the organization to arrive at a diagnosis before deciding on some specialized treatment. The analogy breaks down, however, if one considers that the internist is the prime expert in the diagnosis. He runs tests, asks questions, pokes about, and then delivers a diagnosis and advice. The process consultant, in contrast, attempts to involve the organization in self-diagnosis and enables the organization to give itself sound advice.

A better analogy is to think of the process consultant as a sociotherapist for a system that varies in size and composition from time to time. The concepts of "diagnosis" and "helpful intervention" derive directly from concepts of therapy, especially small-group therapy or training. The major difference between helping a group and consulting for an organization lies in the complexity of the task.

To be an effective process consultant, the person needs diagnostic and intervention skills that are quite different from those used in training or therapy groups. The consultant does not have the environmental supports of a training or therapy setting; he cannot count on the intensive involvement that training groups generate; he cannot even assume a commitment to learning comparable to that of patients or trainees. Through his own interventions, from an ambiguous power base, and in the midst of ongoing work, he must build involvement and commitment, and gain acceptance for the importance of looking at process.

The sociotherapist model suggests itself if one considers

that the consultant is primarily dedicated to helping the system help itself in terms of whatever pathology he may find there. Once an initial contract has been established, the consultant must be prepared to work with whatever he finds, and he must, like the individual therapist, be very careful not to suggest things that will be resisted and not to fall into the trap of thinking he is an expert on that particular organization. All he is expert at is giving help. On the other hand, the sociotherapist model also has limitations in that it suggests pathology. In my experience it is the healthy organization that knows enough to expose itself to help now in order to ensure even greater health in the future. Sick organizations tend to resist help and, alas, PC has no better chance of being introduced in such organizations than any other kind of help.

As a final thought, I would like once again to contrast PC with more standard kinds of consultation models. The standard model is one in which the consultant gives expert advice on how to solve a particular problem that the organization has identified: how to improve production scheduling, how to determine costs, how to obtain marketing information, how to increase productivity, how to select and train certain kinds of personnel, and so on. Even if initial work with the consultant leads to a redefinition of the problem, the consultant's task remains the same: to help develop an expert solution.

The process model, in contrast, starts with the assumption that the organization knows how to solve its particular problems or knows how to get help in solving them, but that it often does not know how to use its own resources effectively either in initial problem formulation or in implementation of solutions. The process model further assumes that inadequate use of internal resources or ineffective implementation result from process problems. By this I mean that people fail to communicate effectively with each other, or develop mistrust, or engage in destructive competition, or punish things that they mean to reward and vice versa, or fail to give feedback, and so on.

The job of the process consultant is to help the organization to solve its own problems by making it aware of organizational processes, the consequences of these processes, and the mechanisms by which they can be changed. The process consultant helps the organization to learn from self-diagnosis and self-intervention. The ultimate concern of the process consultant is the organization's capacity to do for itself what he has done for it. Where the standard consultant is more concerned about passing on his knowledge, the process consultant is concerned about passing on his skills and values.

Appendix A:
Memo I Some Comments
on Internal Auditing
and Control Programs

A. Some Ideas Why Internal Auditing Is Seen As Nonhelpful or As a Source of Tension:

1. Auditors often feel primary loyalty to auditing group rather than company as a whole; they tend, at times, to feel themselves outside of the organization. Managers, on the other hand, feel primary loyalty to organization.
2. Auditors are typically rewarded for finding things wrong, less so for helping people get their work done. Managers, on the other hand, are rewarded for getting the job done, whether things were wrong or not.
3. Auditors tend to be (a) *perfectionists*, and (b) focused on *particular* problems in depth. Managers, on the other hand, tend to be (a) "*satisficers*" rather than maximizers (they tend to look for workable rather than perfect or ideal solutions), and (b) *generalists*, focusing on getting many imperfect things to work together toward getting a job done, rather than perfecting any one part of the job.

4. The auditor's job tempts him to *evaluate* the line operation and to propose solutions. The manager, on the
   other hand, wants *descriptive* (nonevaluative) feedback
   and to design his own solutions.

B. Some Possible Dysfunctional Consequences of Tension Between Line Organization and Auditing Function:

1. Members of the line organization tend to pay attention
   to doing well, primarily in those areas which the auditor
   measures, whether or not those are important to the organizational mission.
2. Members of the line organization put effort into hiding
   problems and imperfections.
3. Management tends to use information about their subordinates in an unintentionally punishing way by immediate inquiries, which gives subordinates the feeling
   of having the boss on their back even while they are
   already correcting the problem.
4. Members of the line organization are tempted to falsify
   and distort information to avoid punishment for being
   "found out," and to avoid having their boss "swoop
   down" on them.
5. *Detailed* information gathered by the auditing function
   tends to be passed too far up the line in both the auditing function and the line organization, making information available to people who are too far removed from
   the problem to know how to evaluate the information.

C. Some Tentative Principles for the Handling of Auditing:

1. *Line involvement:* The more the line organization is involved actively in decisions concerning (a) which areas
   of performance are to be audited, and (b) how the information is to be gathered and to whom it is to be given,

the more helful and effective the auditing function will be.

2. *Horizontal rather than vertical reporting:* The more the auditing information is made available, *first* to the man with the problem (horizontal reporting), then to his immediate boss only if the problem is not corrected, and then only to higher levels in either the line or the auditing group if the problem is still not corrected, the more likely it is that auditing will be effective (because line organizations will be less motivated to hide or falsify information and less likely to feel punished).

3. *Reward for helping rather than policing:* The more the managers in the auditing group reward their subordinates for being *helpful* (based on whether they are being perceived as helpful by the line) rather than being efficient in finding problem areas, the more effective will be the auditing function. (Auditing people tend to be undertrained in how to use audit information in a helpful way; an appropriate reward system should be bolstered by training in how to give help.)

4. *Useful feedback:* The more the auditing information is *relevant* to important operational problems, *timely* in being fed back as soon after problem discovery as possible, and *descriptive* rather than evaluative, the more useful it will be to the line organization.

Appendix B:
Memo II Organization

1. The organization (any organization) can be thought of as having the following components:
   A. *Permanent Systems*
      Examples: product lines, product groups, manufacturing, finance, sales, executive commitee
   B. *Temporary Systems*
      Examples: task forces, review committees, ad hoc problem-solving groups
   C. *Coordinating Systems* (may or may not be permanent)
      Examples: project groups that deliberately cut across product lines (for example, standardization group); production engineering groups that coordinate between some product group and manufacturing; committees charged with functional responsibilities (for example, engineering committee, salary committee, and so on)

   This kind of classification focuses on the issue of whether you put any given function or group, such as marketing, engineering, or programming, into a permanent, temporary, or coordinating role.

The other point about the classification is the identification of weakness in the product line organization as the permanent system, and then the strengthening of the total organization by building appropriate temporary and coordinating systems to offset the weaknesses. For example, if lack of standardization is one of the weaknesses of the product line organization, you build special groups to worry about this, *but they can be temporary groups.*

The basic long-range question, then, is what kind of temporary and/or coordinating systems you need in order to make the product line organization work well.

Appendix C:
Memo III Erosion of Rationality: One Hazard of Internal Competition on Product Planning

1. One major alleged gain of competition is that it increases motivation to win. There is nothing in the ethic of competition, however, that guarantees rationality or concern for high quality (unless you can assume that you need rationality and quality in order to win, an assumption that is often untenable).

2. A second major alleged gain of competition is that several independent problem solvers may produce better solutions than those same problem solvers working together.

3. A major hazard of competition is that, in the desire to win for one's product, one may begin to exaggerate the virtues of one's own product and exaggerate the weaknesses of the competing product. If two or more competitors each begin this process of subtle distortion, it becomes harder and harder to determine the true strengths and weaknesses of each product.

4. A second major hazard of competition is that in the process of selling one's own product solution one becomes emotionally committed to it. This commitment is one reason for the tendency to exaggerate (mentioned

above). A further problem with commitment and loyalty based on competition is that they create an attack-defense type of interaction. One is either selling, advocating, or defending. These types of interaction do not necessarily lead to effective problem solving, because they force both advocate and defender to play up only the good things in their project and to try to hide the weaknesses. In other words, a debate does not encourage true, open communication. Yet can you solve problems rationally without true, open communication?

5. If during the process of competition one or more parties become personally threatened (for example, their own job is threatened by the product decision), the danger arises that the inter*product* competition becomes an inter*personal* competition. If this happens, it becomes harder to make a rational product decision because it implies rejecting one *person*, not merely one *plan*. The issue is not whether this is actually true, but whether or not the participants *feel it to be true.*

6. Once competition becomes inter*personal*, participants increasingly become motivated to play politics and win by behind-the-scenes lobbying, undercutting the adversary, hiding information, making the other person look bad, and so on. Once competition gets to this stage, it is very hard to undo, to get people to work together collaboratively.

7. How can these negative features be avoided while still gaining the advantages of competition?

   A. *Be aware* of the hazards.

   B. *Think through* at what point to switch from competition to collaboration *before* the competitive process has undermined rationality.

   C. *Agree beforehand* at what point you will switch from competition to collaboration. Don't wait until you see the negative symptoms. By that time it may already be too late.

   D. *Make sure everyone knows the ground rules and is willing to play the game that way.*

E. *Keep checking people's feelings* as to whether or not they are beginning to feel threatened. *Build this kind of checking into meetings.* Don't let it become merely "conversation around the water-cooler."

F. *Learn to be flexible;* be able to switch back and forth from competition to collaboration and use each strategy when appropriate.

References

Allen, T. J. *Managing the Flow of Technology.* Cambridge, Mass.: MIT Press, 1977.

Ancona, D. G. Groups in Organizations: Extending Laboratory Models. In C. Hendrick (ed.), *Annual Review of Personality and Social Psychology: Group and Intergroup Processes.* Beverly Hills, Cal.: Sage, 1988.

Bales, R. F. *Interaction Process Analysis.* Reading, Mass.: Addison-Wesley, 1950.

Bales, R. F., and Cohen, S. P. *SYMLOG.* New York: Free Press, 1979.

Bennis, W., and Nanus, B. *Leaders.* New York: Harper & Row, 1985.

Birdwhistell, R. L. "Paralanguage: Twenty-five Years After Sapir." In H. Brosin (ed.), *Lectures on Experimental Psychiatry.* Pittsburgh: University of Pittsburgh Press, 1961.

Blake, R. R., and Mouton, J. S. "Reactions to Intergroup Competition Under Win–Lose Conditions." *Man. Sci.,* 1961, 7, 420–435.

——. "Overcoming Group Warfare." *Harvard Business Review,* Nov.–Dec. 1984, no. 6, 98–108.

Bradford, L. P.; Gibb, J. R.; and Benne, K. D. (eds.). *T-group Theory and Laboratory Method.* New York: Wiley, 1964.

Carter, L.; Haythorn, W.; Meirowitz, B.; and Lanzetta, J. "A Note on a New Technique of Interaction Recording." *J. Abn. Soc. Psych.*, 1951, 46, 258–260.

Chapple, E. D. "Measuring Human Relations: An Introduction to the Study of Interaction of Individuals." *Gen. Psych. Mono.*, 1940, 22, 3–147.

Dalton, M. *Men Who Manage.* New York: Wiley, 1959.

Hall, E. T. *The Silent Language.* Garden City, N.Y.: Doubleday, 1959.

Harvey, J. B. "The Abilene Paradox: The Managment of Agreement." *Organizational Dynamics*, summer, 1974.

Lewin, K. "Frontiers in Group Dynamics." *Human Relations*, 1947, 1, 5–41.

Scheflen, A. E. "Quasi-Courtship Behavior in Psychotherapy." *Psychiatry*, 1965, 28, 245–255.

Schein, E. H. *Organizational Psychology.* Engelwood Cliffs, N.J.: Prentice-Hall, 1965. Third edition, 1980.

––––. *Organizational Culture and Leadership.* San Francisco: Jossey-Bass, 1985.

––––. *Process Consultation: Volume II.* Reading, Mass.: Addison-Wesley, 1987a.

––––. *The Clinical Perspective in Fieldwork.* Newbury Park, Cal.: Sage, 1987b.

Schein, E. H., and Bennis, W. G. *Personal and Organizational Change Through Group Methods.* New York: Wiley, 1965.

Sherif, M.; Harvey, O. J.; White, B. J.; Hood, W. R.; and Sherif, C. W. *Intergroup Conflict and Cooperation.* Norman: University of Oklahoma Book Exchange, 1961.

Tannenbaum, R., and Schmidt, W. H. "How to Choose a Leadership Pattern." *Harvard Business Review*, 1958, 36, 95–101.

White, R., and Lippitt, R. "Leader Behavior and Member Reactions in Three Social Climates." In D. Cartwright and A. Zander (eds.), *Group Dynamics.* White Plains, N.Y.: Row-Peterson, 1953.